"Jack Graham has touched many lives, stirs hope and develops character. His any shelf."

Max Lucad

"Is there any greater gift than the incor Spirit? I agree with Jack Graham that the answer is no. It is the Holy Spirit who turns quivering cowards into bold martyrs. It is the Holy Spirit who transforms sleepwalkers into wide-awake witnesses for him. It is the Holy Spirit who powers us up to further usher in the kingdom of God! Get the themes of this book in you. And together, let's change the world for good."

Tony Evans, Co-founder and Senior Pastor,
Oak Cliff Bible Fellowship

"*Powering Up* is jam-packed with nuggets of biblical truth from the Source of power—the Lord Jesus Christ. Jack Graham enlightens us to the dangers of culture-followers and how Christ-followers can be obedient to the Great Commission without compromise in order to win the lost to the Savior of the world. My prayer is that this book will illuminate minds and hearts with God's electrifying light."

Franklin Graham, President and CEO,
Samaritan's Purse and Billy Graham Evangelistic Association

"*Powering Up* is timely, practical, well-illustrated, conclusive, and trans-formative if one will take it to heart. My husband grabbed it and didn't take a breather until he had read nearly two hundred pages! I heartily recommend it."

Kay Arthur, Founder, Precept Ministries

"Fuel efficiency is critical to our cars, but what about our spiritual lives? Dr. Jack Graham's latest book, *Powering Up*, is a must read for anyone seeking to reach full potential from God. With intriguing stories and touching insights, *Powering Up* will reboot your relationship with God and help you live the life he wants."

Mike Huckabee, former governor of Arkansas

"Through his ministry, Jack Graham has introduced thousands to Christ and discipled countless leaders in the Christian community. In *Powering Up*, Jack shares personal testimonies that illustrate how Christ-centered living fulfills God's purpose for our time on earth."

U. S. Senator Kay Bailey Hutchison, Texas

"When Jack Graham speaks or writes, I am all ears. *Powering Up* is his most important book yet. Get ready for a supernatural infusion of spiri-tual vigor and life-changing power."

Pat Williams, Senior Vice President,
Orlando Magic; author of *What Are You Living for?*

"Biblical, practical, and motivating! If you long to reconnect with God in a way that will make a real difference in your life, open this book and start reading."

Chip Ingram, Teaching Pastor, Living on the Edge; author of *Good to Great in God's Eyes* and *Effective Parenting in a Defective World*

"Proverbs teaches us, 'as a man thinketh in his heart, so is he.' Jack Graham challenges us to give careful thought to our ways, that we may think and live like the Savior we worship and love."

Daniel L. Akin, President,
Southeastern Baptist Theological Seminary

"One of the greatest pastors and finest men I know has written a book that literally pulsates with the power he talks about! If you want a God-empowered change in your life, read this book—you will indeed be powered up!"

James Merritt, Pastor, Cross Pointe Church, Duluth, Georgia

"Jack Graham doles out massive helpings of hope in this book. This is what you've been looking for if you want to see change in your life, especially if you've been held down by the grip of past failures. The insights Jack records here are not the same old tired and predictable notions of so many other lofty tomes. This book is deeply biblical and therefore very practical. You'll find here a no-nonsense approach to living and *enjoying* a Spirit-empowered life."

Skip Heitzig, Senior Pastor, Calvary of Albuquerque

"There are a lot of self-help books on the market right now. In fact if you google 'Self-Help Books,' you will come up with twenty-two million hits. That's a lot of information about developing yourself. How do you determine the truly helpful information and the truly unhelpful and possibly even harmful information? You look and see if it is founded and based upon the truth of God's Word. Jack Graham's book *Powering Up* is founded upon the principles of a Spirit-filled life and it comes straight from the Word of God. If you are longing for a life of fulfillment and fruitfulness, I can, without reservation, recommend this powerful and practical book!"

Jonathan Falwell, Senior Pastor,
Thomas Road Baptist Church, Lynchburg, Virginia

"I found *Powering Up* to be a powerful refresher in the basics of Christian discipleship, compelling for me as a believer for many years but just as applicable to someone new to the faith. *Powering Up* is thoroughly biblical, communicated in the practical, relevant, and common-sense approach that characterizes Jack Graham's pastoral ministry. It is not difficult to appreciate the Prestonwood Baptist Church phenomenon after reading Dr. Graham's latest contribution to the body of Christ."

Edward G. Atsinger III, Chief Executive Officer,
Salem Communications Corporation, Camarillo, California

POWERING UP

THE FULFILLMENT AND FRUIT
OF A GOD-FUELED LIFE

JACK GRAHAM

CROSSWAY BOOKS

WHEATON, ILLINOIS

Cover design: The Design Works Group
Interior design and typesetting: Lakeside Design Plus

First printing, 2009
Printed in the United States of America

Unless otherwise indicated, Scripture quotations are taken from the ESV®. (*The Holy Bible: English Standard Version*), copyright© 2001 by Crossway Bibles, a publishing ministry of Good News Publishers. Used by permission. All rights reserved.

    Scripture quotations marked KJV are from the King James Version of the Bible.

    Scripture quotations marked MSG are from *The Message*. Copyright © (*The Holy Bible: English Standard Version)*, copyright by Eugene H. Peterson 1993, 1994, 1995, 1996, 2000, 2001, 2002. Used by permission of NavPress Publishing Group.

    Scripture quotations marked NASB are from *The New American Standard Bible.*® Copyright © The Lockman Foundation 1960, 1962, 1963, 1968, 1971, 1972, 1973, 1975, 1977, 1995. Used by permission.

    Scripture references marked NIV are from *The Holy Bible: New International Version.*® Copyright © 1973, 1978, 1984 by International Bible Society. Used by permission of Zondervan Publishing House. All rights reserved. The "NIV" and "New International Version" trademarks are registered in the United States Patent and Trademark Office by International Bible Society. Use of either trademark requires the permission of International Bible Society.

    Scripture references marked NKJV are from *The New King James Version*. Copyright © 1982, Thomas Nelson, Inc. Used by permission.

    Scripture references marked NLT are from *The Holy Bible, New Living Translation*, copyright © 1996. Used by permission of Tyndale House Publishers, Inc., Wheaton, Ill., 60189. All rights reserved.

ISBN: 978-1-4335-0658-1
PDF ISBN: 978-1-4335-0659-8
Mobipocket ISBN: 978-1-4335-0660-4

Library of Congress Cataloging-in-Publication Data
Graham, Jack, 1950-
    Powering up : the fulfillment and fruit of a God-fueled life / Jack Graham.
       p. cm.
    Includes bibliographical references.
    ISBN 978-1-4335-0658-1 (tpb)
    1. Christian life. I. Title.

    BV4501.3.G733 2009
    248.4—dc22

                                            2008048763

SH			19	18	17	16	15	14	13	12	11	10	09
14	13	12	11	10	9	8	7	6	5	4	3	2	1

To Joan Frost,
the mother of my beloved, Deb,
and the grandmother of our children.
Your beautiful spirit and faithful heart
encourage all who know you.

The conversion of a soul is the miracle of a moment;
the manufacture of a saint is the task of a lifetime.

Alan Redpath, *The Making of a Man of God*

Contents

Acknowledgments   9

Introduction: More than a Benevolent Jelly Bean   11

Part One: Wonder-Working You

1 A Swift Kick in the Dish   19
   Returning to the Life You Were Born to Live

2 A Profile of Powered-Up Living   33
   The Hero's Welcome We'll One Day Receive

3 Breathing Native Air   45
   Inspiration Straight from the Spirit of God

Part Two: Rules of Engagement

4 Praying with Potency   61
   Faith in More than GPS

5 Marching to a Divine Drumbeat   77
   How to Stay in Sync with the Spirit of God

6 Speaking Wisdom's Words   93
   The Case for Being a Camel Not Stuck in a Zoo

Part Three: By-Products of Being Empowered

7 Mind Matters   111
   Firstfruits of the God-Fueled Life

8 We Are Our Brother's Keeper   141
   Real-Deal Disciples in a Fraud-Filled Age

9 Passion Fruit   171
   Reining in What Seeks to Break Free

10 The Empowered Church   207
   Christian Community the Way God Intended It to Be

   Afterword: Careful Thought to Your Ways   217
   Notes   221

Acknowledgments

Once again I am grateful to have had the opportunity to publish with my friends at Crossway Books. Each project we share serves to further convince me of their character and of their commitment to strengthen God's people with Scripture and its application to daily life. Integrity and quality are Crossway's distinctions, and I am so pleased to be one of their authors.

This book never would have found its way into your hands without the excellent creative work of Ashley Wiersma. She took my words and shaped them into a strong and vibrant book. With an amazing work ethic and a firm commitment to sharing God's truth, she handed me the opportunity to bring this message to you. Thank you, Ashley. You are a delight!

The heart and soul of this book contains messages first delivered at my beloved Prestonwood Baptist Church. I am always overwhelmed by the goodness of God, which allows me to be their pastor. Thank you, church, for your love and devotion to Christ and for so faithfully modeling the content of this work.

I would be remiss if I did not also thank the team at PowerPoint Ministries for "powering up" with me in our efforts to spread the gospel around the world. Our radio, television, and Internet ministry provides us the daily honor of making a difference in so many lives, and I am grateful for their constant support.

My wife, Deb, is my greatest encourager. Thank you for being the love of my life and for blessing us with a fantastic family that loves to serve Christ.

Introduction

More than a Benevolent Jelly Bean

The joys of being a pastor are innumerable, but there is one joy that sits high above all others, and it is the joy of seeing a human life transformed by the presence and power of God.

A career criminal gets set free.

An addict finds *real* release.

An adulterer embraces faithfulness.

A liar finds the Truth.

A cynic learns to care.

I could serve another forty years in ministry, and I would *never* grow weary of seeing life-change like that.

Clearly, every story of redemption is a miraculous and magnificent tale. But some testimonies are so dramatic in nature and so unexpected in outcome that they seem to prove God's power in fresh and unusual ways.

Lee Strobel's is such a story.

Our church, Prestonwood Baptist, in Plano, Texas, hosted my good friend Lee recently and learned that although he had been cynical toward God since his teenage years, by God's grace Lee didn't stay in that state.

Lee Strobel was trained in the legal profession and ultimately worked as an editor for the *Chicago Tribune* where people prided themselves on being skeptical and on requiring two confirmed sources before printing a single fact. Not surprisingly, his disdain for things of "faith" ballooned. "The idea of an all-knowing, all-loving, all-powerful 'creator of the universe' was an *absurd* concept to me," Lee said of his posture during those years. "It wasn't even worth my time to learn more, because in my view there was no way that something called 'God' could create people. No, *people* created *God* because they were afraid of death. They created a benevolent jelly bean in the sky, complete with a fantasy they called 'heaven,' so that they could feel better about their lives now and less fearful about their death sometime in the future. That is what I believed. And nothing was going to change my mind."

Lee admits that his greatest value in life was to keep himself happy at all costs, to experience *maximum* personal pleasure. That lifestyle led him down an immoral path of drunkenness, profanity, narcissism, and ultimately self-destruction. "I had an incredible amount of rage brewing inside," Lee admits, "because I was always after some 'better high.' I wanted to reach that next level of pleasure, but I never seemed to find it. The pursuit absolutely enraged me."

With soberness in his voice, Lee explained to our congregation how his anger affected his home life. "One day my wife was sitting in the living room with our young daughter, Alison. Something set me off, and out of sheer anger, I reared back and kicked a hole in the wall, right in front of them. They both fell apart in tears, but I was numb to their reaction. It's just who I was back then."

Lee's wife was agnostic when they were married, but she would eventually meet a believer who would tell her of Jesus' love. "Lee, I have decided to become a follower of Jesus Christ," she would tell her husband one evening over dinner. Which caused Lee's head to spin. "It was the worst possible news I could have gotten," he later said. "I thought she'd turn into a sexually repressed prude. I thought she'd spend every night of the week serving poor people on Skid Row. And that is *not* what I signed up for when I married her."

But in the months that followed, Lee noticed positive changes in his wife. Her heart softened, and the relationship improved. She was winsome and attractive and kind. Wooed by his wife's new demeanor, Lee actually said yes when she invited him to come to church with her one Sunday morning.

The talk was titled "Basic Christianity," and it shattered Lee's misconceptions about what Christians truly believe. "I walked out of that place with two thoughts," Lee said. "First of all, I was still an atheist. The pastor was good, but he wasn't *about* to convince me that God exists!" But the second thought Lee had was that if the pastor's claims regarding Christ *were* in fact true, they would have huge implications for his life.

Lee decided to use his training—both legal and journalistic—to systematically investigate whether there was any credibility to this thing called Christianity. "One Sunday afternoon, I did what I was taught at Yale," he said. "I took out a yellow legal pad and put a line down the center. On one side I put the negative evidence for Jesus being the unique Son of God; on the other side I put the positive evidence that I'd found. After pages and pages of notes, finally I put down my pen. As I looked at my findings, I realized that it would have required more faith for me to maintain my atheism than to become a Christian. In that moment I realized that based on the historical record, I really did believe that Jesus is the unique Son of God; he *claimed* it, and then he *proved* it by returning from the dead."

But then what?

Lee remembered a Bible verse a friend had once pointed out to him, John 1:12, which says, "As many as received Him, to them He gave the right to become children of God, even to those who believe in His name" (NASB).

He had the "believe" part down but still had to "receive." In an act of surrender that must have made God's face break into a wide smile, Lee Strobel, career sinner and poster boy for immoral living, got down on his knees and poured out a confession to his heavenly Father.

"For the first time in my life," he later explained, "that 'something greater' I had been straining for I finally could reach. I reached out and found the hand of Jesus"—the Jesus who is who he says he is, the Jesus who is alive today.

From that day forward, Lee began to open up his life to the leadership of Jesus Christ. Not overnight, but certainly over time God began to reshape Lee's worldview and his character and his values and his parenting practices. Over time he began to change *everything* for the good.

The first five years of Lee's daughter's life were influenced by a dad who was drunk and angry and brash. But as Lee began to walk in newness of life, her five-year-old eyes saw her daddy's life changed. A few months into his radical transformation, the little girl walked up to her mom and said, "Mommy, I want God to do for me what he's done for Daddy." And at age five she too became a follower of Jesus.

Oh, the power of a transformed life.

God often uses amazing stories like this one, stories of men and women who have been captured and captivated and changed by the power of his presence, so that we will see him for who he really is.

The Bible is *full* of stories like this, but one of my all-time favorites involves a beggar and a gate called "Beautiful."

In the third chapter of Acts we meet a man who was born disabled. He could not walk and had never chased a dream. Ultimately his caretakers figured the only way he could carve out a living would be to beg for money. Each day somebody—his brother or uncle or another family member or a friend—would take him to the gate just outside the temple area, which was the place of worship, so he could beg passers by for a little aid.

For forty years this man lay at the gate called Beautiful, crying out "alms for the poor, alms for the poor" as he tried to survive another empty day. But one day along came two men who were filled with the power of God and as a result would change *everything* for this man.

The apostles Peter and John were on their way to worship, and as they walked along, the beggar at the gate called Beautiful cried out to them and asked them for money.

Suddenly Peter stopped walking. With John at his side, he stared down at the disabled man and said, "Sir, look at us."

It's possible that this man had not looked up at a human face in four decades. Most likely his head had always stayed down, his eyes had always focused on the same slab of pavement as hurried feet rushed by, his heart had always been pulverized by the same insults and scathing words of rejection.

"*Look* at you?" the man must have thought. "Me? Look at *you*?" Pushing aside his disbelief, the man craned his neck back, directed his eyes skyward, and looked upon Peter and John in anticipation of receiving their alms. But he would get something far better than that.

Acts 3:6 says that Peter looked upon the man and said, "I have no silver and gold, but what I do have I give to you. In the name of Jesus Christ of Nazareth, rise up and walk!"

And with that, a brawny fisherman reached down and lifted up not a disabled man but a healed one. His feet and ankles had been made strong, and leaping up, he stood and began to walk straight into the temple with them, hopping and cheering and praising his God. Bondage and brokenness and baggage had been replaced by the miraculous filling-up of the unparalleled power of God.

⏻

At first blush Lee Strobel and the lame man seem so different. One was a successful cynic, the other a bedraggled beggar. One searched for God out of spite, the other out of sheer desperation. But it is their similarity, not their differences, that strikes me the most. Both men shared the same need—the need for forgiveness and purpose and mind-blowing, wonder-working *power*. And both would discover that their need could only be met in God—the God who breaks bondages, who answers prayers, who gives hope to the hopeless, who *utterly changes lives*.

Regardless of who you are—what sins have beset you, what dreams fire you up, how you plan at the present moment to live the rest of your life—you need the power of God too, the God who is *far* from being a benevolent jelly bean in the sky. As Psalm 3:3 says, he is "the lifter of my [and your] head." He is the healer of our hearts. He is the only true catalyst for change. And he longs to transform you today. What Peter said to the lame man two thousand years ago is what I say to you now: "Rise up. By the power of God, rise up and walk in newness of life."

PART ONE

Wonder-Working You

The fact that some hundred-year-old songs are still sung in churches all over the world today tells me that their sentiment continues to strike a chord with their singers. "There Is Power in the Blood" is one such song, and regardless of your particular age and your particular spiritual experience, its chorus is probably familiar to you. "There is pow'r," it begins, "pow'r, wonder-working pow'r in the blood of the Lamb; there is pow'r, pow'r, wonder-working pow'r in the precious blood of the Lamb."[1]

The hymn provides such a catchy tune that it's easy to belt out the words without letting them sink into your heart. But sink in they must, lest we miss one of the greatest truths we can know in this life: the ultimate form of power—*wonder-working power* even—is found in God and in God alone, and when we willingly, joyfully, expectantly surrender to our Power-Broker's leadings, we will live powered-up lives every day.

1

A Swift Kick in the Dish

Returning to the Life You Were Born to Live

There's nothing like the first game of a brand-new NFL season. Last year's Super Bowl is now a distant memory, and the only action you've known for months on end is of the verbal variety. There has been talk of trades and talk of retirements and talk of the draft and talk of preseason games, which everyone knows count for zilch in the grand scheme of all things football. But then, finally, the day dawns when all that talk ceases and the ball is snapped for real. Everyone has zero wins, zero losses, and for the only moment during the whole season when this is true, your team has as much of a fighting chance as anyone to take home the big prize. What a rush!

You can imagine, then, how disheartened I was when I stood in front of my TV a couple of Septembers ago, remote in hand, anxious to set my TiVo to record the NFL-season-opening battle between the Saints and the Colts and saw my screen blank out. I pushed a few buttons, and it sputtered and spat. I pushed a few more buttons. More sputters, more spit. We have a dish on the side of our house, so I thought, *Oh, I know what to do here. I'll just restart the unit that controls the entire satellite system.* It drew on the full extent of my technological knowledge, that single act of turning a little black box off, then on again, but it worked. And as the picture hummed beautifully back to life, I saw two words appear on-screen: *Powering Up.*

I stared at that phrase for a few seconds, thinking, *Wouldn't it be great if it were this easy to power me back up when I am behaving a little beneath my potential? What if every Christ-follower, for that matter, could just push a simple button when his or her picture was fuzzy or the signal was weak?* We all lack clarity and consistency from time to time. We all need help maintaining a predictable picture of what the watching world needs to see, an image that accurately and faithfully portrays the character of Christ. Maybe a swift kick in the dish, a reboot, and a fresh shot at powering up could do the trick, if only that could occur in the spiritual realm.

Ready for a Reboot

If you're like most Christ-followers I know, you've walked through a season or two when you really could have used a restart button. Maybe you're in such a season right now: your picture has been breaking up and sputtering and spitting, and you know that the life you're living is not the life God wishes for you to live. You're fading in and out of obedience to his commands, and therefore fading in and out of true freedom, causing the people around you to wonder whether or not you really do follow Christ. You're weary of the superficial and in desperate need of a massive dose of something supernatural that will enable you to face life's struggles head-on and flourish in God's goodness for days and years to come, but you just don't know where to turn for help.

If that is true for you, then you are not alone. I have served in a local church setting for nearly forty years, and if there is one thing I've heard Christians of all ages, races, backgrounds, and traditions say they desire more than anything else, it is *the certainty that the power of God really can make a difference in their lives.*

Think for a moment about your spiritual journey to date. There have probably been some highs and some lows, but as you consider the questions below, only take into account where you see yourself now.

On a scale of 1 to 10—1 meaning "sputtering along" and 10 meaning "absolutely prevailing," where do you rank your spiritual life?

What are three primary factors—such as habits, practices, relationships, assumptions, and so forth—that play a role in how you answered?

They look at their sorry circumstances and their below-potential behavior and want to know that Jesus really can change their hearts, their habits, their desires, their patterns, and their pain. They want to know that there is enough power for them to overcome the work of the enemy in their personal lives and the forces of evil flowing through the world at large, that there is enough power for them to *prevail.* To their concerns—and perhaps to yours as well—I say, there is! There is *plenty* of power awaiting you, life-changing, habit-altering, pain-alleviating power. It's what powering up is all about, as even Jesus' earliest followers could attest.

Common Men, an Uncommon Opportunity

Two thousand years ago a large group of believers led by twelve men qualified as the least likely people to change the world. They were known as "disciples"—handpicked followers who would co-labor with Christ. These were rural, ordinary folk. Common men, you might say. They were sometimes rude and sometimes crude and sometimes full of rage. One of them, John, was known as a "son of thunder" and had a bit of an agitated temperament to get over before he'd experience life in all its fullness. Another,

21

Peter, often said the wrong thing at the wrong time. Occasionally he'd say the right thing, but it was still at the wrong time.

When Jesus was nailed to the cross, these once-devoted followers caved in to their fears about being associated with a dead king and chose to flee their Master's presence. They ran and hid in the shadows and denied having anything to do with the Messiah. Even after Jesus was raised from the dead, the disciples wondered about his power. Sure, they *said* they believed in the risen Christ, but relying on a crucified leader's power to continue on with the mission they had been given? Well, that was a different proposition altogether.

Jesus' first followers were uneducated, untrained, and unfit for the massive opportunity they would be ultimately invited to seize. "I want you to go into all the world and make disciples," Jesus would say. And incredibly they said yes. Armed with nothing but that twelve-word directive, the small band of brothers eyed their upside-down world and engaged wholeheartedly in the task of setting it right.

Despite having no financial resources, no elaborate buildings, no satellite technology, no cameras, no media to broadcast their movement, and no ability to produce PR flyers advertising their events, the disciples thrived in their mission for one reason and one reason alone: they had something that was better than all of the bells and whistles put together—the *transforming* power of God in their lives.

Because they looked to God's power for their strength, they beat the odds.

Because they looked to God's power for their strength, they stood firm against opposition.

Because they looked to God's power for their strength, they persisted amid persecution.

Because they looked to God's power for their strength, they gained some *serious* kingdom ground, living life precisely as it was meant to be lived.

I think there's a lesson here for you and me both.

The God-Sized Gift

In the first chapter of the book of Acts we read that Jesus gathered his disciples around him on the Mount of Olives, which stands even today, just due east of the city of Jerusalem. Their heads were probably still spinning as they considered the roller-coaster ride of experiences they'd known during the three years they had followed Jesus. They had felt the joys of absorbing his firsthand ministry, the sorrow of witnessing the horrible ordeal of the cross, and the elation of knowing he was now resurrected.

Their Lord had chosen them, taught them, loved them, and prepared them and now was commissioning them just before he ascended into heaven. The disciples barely had time to grieve their Master's impending departure, though, before they were given a promise—a promise that although it was true that Christ was leaving, "another" was coming to take his place (John 14:16). "[The apostle] John baptized with water," Jesus would say on that mount just forty days after his miraculous resurrection, "but you will be baptized with the Holy Spirit not many days from now" (Acts 1:5). And what a baptism it was! The first verses of Acts 2 describe the fulfillment of that promise this way:

> When the day of Pentecost arrived, they were all together in one place. And suddenly there came from heaven a sound like a mighty rushing wind, and it filled the entire house where they were sitting. And divided tongues as of fire appeared to them and rested on each one of them. And they were all filled with the Holy Spirit and began to speak in other tongues as the Spirit gave them utterance. (vv. 1–4)

This was the Day of Pentecost—the day when the Spirit of God, by way of three miracles, took up residence in every believer, and the church of Jesus Christ was officially born.

The Miracle of Sound

The first miracle of Pentecost was the miracle of sound, for those gathered heard "a sound like a mighty rushing wind."

The word for "spirit" in the New Testament is *pneuma*, which means "breath." "Spirit of God" is literally, "the breath of God." So when this particular wind blew in and around that throng of believers, it represented the *life of God*, the very *respiration of God* now imparted to them, feeble and frail human beings.

The Miracle of Sight

But not only was there a miracle of sound, there was also a miracle of sight. You could say things went nuclear at Pentecost that day. A gigantic ball of fire exploded, and divided flames from its core danced atop believers' heads, human candles quite literally ignited by the Holy Spirit.

It is a common image in Scripture, this idea of God as a consuming fire. When God gets involved, fire is often involved too. Remember the burning bush? Moses came to that bush, and the thing kept on burning and burning—a manifestation of God's presence there. The same was true at Pentecost. Symbolized by a raging fire, God was with them in fullness of presence and in fullness of power. God, the grand consumer, cleanser, changer of *everything*.

The Miracle of Speech

There was a third miracle that day at Pentecost, and it was the miracle of speech. People from all over the world had gathered, and suddenly it was as if God hit his divine fast-forward button, and the gospel was disseminated to all tribes in one fell swoop. Instead of the good news reaching the nations, the nations had reached the good news. And they heard it simultaneously and in their native tongues, living languages spoken in their own unique dialects. Talk about a supernatural sensory experience! "My power I will leave with you," Jesus had promised in essence. And with the ultimate love language now on their tongues, power is exactly what those early believers possessed.

Wonder-Working Power

According to Paul in the book of Ephesians, the power that Christ was referring to a few days before that Day of Pentecost

(Acts 1:8) was the same power that brought him out of the grave (1:19–20). The Greek word that the apostle uses—*dunamis* (pronounced doo-na-mis)—is the word from which we get the English word *dynamite* and reminds us that there indeed is explosive power and, more importantly perhaps, *dynamic* power in the work of the Holy Spirit. When led by the Spirit, a *continual* source of strength and energy flows through the life of the believer.

How does this divine strength and energy—this *dunamis*—show up? Take a look at the promises of Scripture: in Romans 15:13, we are filled with hope because of *dunamis*. In Ephesians 3:16, *dunamis* equips us to serve God successfully. According to this same passage, in verse 20, *dunamis* allows us to do more than we can possibly imagine. According to Ephesians 6, *dunamis* enables us to overcome the enemy. According to Colossians 1:11, *dunamis* gives us perseverance in the tests and trials of life and the discipline to know righteousness each day. In Colossians 1:29, we're told that *dunamis* causes us to work energetically for God. In 1 Peter 1:5, *dunamis* protects us. Second Peter 1:3 says that *dunamis* provides everything we need to live godly lives.

Jesus would tell his disciples, "These works that I have done, you will do, and greater works than these, you will do."[1] Can you imagine how stunned they must have been when they learned that all that Jesus had done was only the beginning and that they would be doing something even "greater"? This is the heartbeat of the book of Acts, which is simply a series of great works or "acts" that bear testimony to the power of the church when its people are fueled by *dunamis*. Even today the great works persist: whenever the sun shines on a corner of the world, it shines on someone preaching the gospel. Wherever the moon casts her beams, she illuminates someone saying a word for God. Twenty-four hours a day, seven days a week, the good news is being proclaimed. What joy this must bring our Father!

The Ultimate Before and After

What was true for those believers gathered at Pentecost remains true for us today: when the Holy Spirit infiltrates a human life, *dunamis* power starts to flow. And its first objective is accomplishing the renovating work of transformation. Spirit-led believers experience this transformation as they move from emptiness to fullness, from failure to faith, and from fear to courage. The end result? It's the *ultimate* before and after.

From Emptiness to Fullness

Immediately after the trio of sensory miracles on the day of Pentecost—sound, sight, and speech—Acts 2 says that the apostle Peter preached a powerful message to all who were gathered, culminating with a crystal-clear invitation to have their spiritual emptiness filled with Jesus Christ. "Repent and be baptized every one of you in the name of Jesus Christ for the forgiveness of your sins," verse 38 says, "and you will receive the gift of the Holy Spirit."

People wanted to know what to do to be saved, what to do to have their lives transformed. "Repent!" Peter exclaimed. "Turn from the direction you were headed, and start walking a new path. Stop sinning, follow Jesus Christ, and the Holy Spirit is yours."

I still can't read those words without getting choked up because I remember all too well what my life was like before I turned from the direction I was headed and started walking a new path. You're reading the words of a man who knows he's saved. I've done exactly what the Scriptures tell us to do in responding to the invitation to repent and receive Christ, and as a result the Spirit of God circulates through me, testifying that I belong to him and securing me in my faith. The fullness of God's presence and power does not come through good deeds. It does not come through church membership. It does not even come through growing up in a godly family. It comes, my friend, *only* through salvation in Christ.

From Failure to Faith

Transformation also means moving from failure and defeat to faith and spiritual fire. The believers at Pentecost lacked faith. They lacked fervor. They knew their past sins well and wondered if God could ever use people like them, given their significant track record of failure. I can certainly relate. On more than a few occasions I've asked God the question, "Is it *really* possible that I can achieve your mission when I'm this far from being perfect?"

POWER POINT

> What infractions have sidelined you in life thus far? How would your life be different if Christ were given complete freedom to remove those sinful patterns for you now?

So many believers stay planted on the spiritual bench because they have failed God in some way and wonder if the infraction will leave them permanently sidelined. They have lackluster prayer lives. They're enslaved to habits they cannot break. They're in bondage to sin they cannot shake. They can't control their thought life, they can't control their mouths, they can't control their morals, they can't control their appetites. They're living in defeat and at great distance from the God who created them and loves them, constantly teetering on the brink of spiritual despondency because they don't realize that with God's presence comes his promise to renew us day by day, to fire us up moment by moment. Regardless of our past. Regardless of our sin.

God chooses to use the foolish in this world, failures and sinfulness and all, in order to shame the wise. He empowers us, he equips us, he tasks us, and he gives us great success, all for the purpose of showing himself strong. He provides strength in the midst of struggle, joy amid mourning, love to fend off fear. Think about this with me for a moment: when God uses people like you and me who are utterly undeserving and unworthy of being used, and he accomplishes *magnificent* things through us, who do you suppose gets the glory? God does!

When we as God's people realize a measure of success in ministry, it is never due to our talents or abilities or wittiness or exceptional planning. Success *always* flows from God's hand, and God's alone. It is "not by might, nor by power," Zechariah 4:6 says, "but by my Spirit, says the LORD of hosts."

When I was a young seminary student, the church I served in Ft. Worth had a great revival. It was amazing! People came to Christ left and right, and those of us who witnessed it were floating on a spiritual high like none we'd ever known. The next day I walked into my evangelism class, taught by a man I greatly admire to this day, Dr. Roy Fish. He asked me how I was doing, and I responded with a puffed-up chest and a hefty dose of piety, "We're all rejoicing in this incredible revival we had over at the church!"

To my surprise, Dr. Fish wasn't impressed. His gaze searing my eyes, he said, "You'd better rejoice in the *Reviver*, not in the revival." He turned to head toward his lectern as I nodded silently and sort of slumped off to the back row.

I was a bit humiliated, but Dr. Fish was right. Our spiritual victories must always be credited to the only One worthy of our praise—the great reviver and transformer of our failures, Jesus Christ.

From Fear to Courage

From emptiness to fullness, from failure to faith, and finally, *from fear to courage*—transformation's work accomplishes them all.

As I mentioned, immediately following the astonishing impartation of the Holy Spirit, Peter began to preach with boldness previously not possessed. This is the same Peter, mind you, who had denied Christ on three separate occasions. But because of the Spirit's transforming ways, a wimp was turned into a warrior for God.

Later on Peter and John were arrested and were beaten to within an inch of their lives and were told never to speak in the name of Jesus again. In Acts 4:13 city officials who observed the boldness of Peter and John admitted that these men must have had an encounter with Christ. How else could untrained and unintelligent men be so courageous and bold? That's a question only the Holy Spirit can answer. So how does such transformation take place? Where is the relevance to us today? Let's keep going.

Transformation for Today

On any sports team, it's the coach's responsibility to outline a strategy, come up with a game plan, and empower the team to execute it. One of my all-time favorite coaches is the late, great Tom Landry, who served for nearly three decades as head coach of the championship-rich Dallas Cowboys. This beloved brother in Christ was a faithful man who used his professional platform to share Jesus with as many people as possible. One day a reporter asked Coach Landry, "How do you do it? How do you keep producing winning teams year after year? How do you take a group of individuals with their own agendas and forge them into a unified unit, building them into a team that wins so consistently?"

Tom Landry replied, "My job is to get men to do what they don't want to do in order to achieve what they always wanted to achieve." Of course, what football players wanted to achieve always involved winning a championship title or a Super Bowl victory. And many, many times Tom Landry prepared his team to do just that.

Jesus knows how to prepare his team to win, too. While he was still here on earth, it was as if he huddled his team around him and said, "Guys, you only need to know two plays to power up and make this thing called life work well: wait, and go."

Play #1: Wait

The first thing Jesus asks his players to do is to *wait*. "Do not depart from Jerusalem," he told his disciples in essence in Acts 1:4, "but *wait* for the coming of the Spirit." In response to their Lord's request, the disciples waited, but not idly. Rather, they did what nobody would expect a rough, tough, manly group of men to do—they hosted a prayer meeting! A hundred and twenty of them gathered in an upstairs room and waited for God's Spirit to come.

POWER POINT

Do you find it easy or difficult to wait on God before moving forward with a determined course of action? In what areas might God be asking you to wait on him today?

We are wise to do the same. Before we engage, we must disengage. Before we rush out, knocking things over and tearing things up for Jesus, we must be sure that the Spirit of God is filling and fueling our lives. Before we *go*, we must *wait*.

Play #2: Go

But there was a second part to the game plan. When Jesus rallied his team for the big game, he said, "You will receive power when the Holy Spirit has come upon you, and you will be my witnesses."[2]

"*My witnesses*"—that's the mission you and I have been given. And no matter what age we may be in the faith—a rookie believer or a veteran—we are responsible to carry out the mission of Christ. Even a senior saint is held to this; there is no such thing as retirement from the work of Jesus. The word *retired* is not found in Christ's vocabulary. Indeed, we are witnesses of great things: we know of our Lord's death and his burial, we know of his resurrection, we know of the transformation that has occurred in our lives. And *this* is the message we are entrusted to share, a message we'll explore further in Chapter 6.

Ready to Power Up?

There is no human explanation for what happened in those early days of the church as the Holy Spirit revolutionized and revitalized reluctant men and women, transforming them into bold, brave-hearted witnesses for Christ who would cause the gospel to explode throughout first-century Jerusalem. The events of the book of Acts are only explicable in terms of God's propensity to take common men and women and accomplish highly uncommon things, all in the name of powering up. These followers were committed to sharing the gospel of Christ and to living lives worthy of their calling. And with God's power, they did just that.

Maybe you are one who wonders, "How do I live out this thing called the Christian life? How can I be part of changing the world for good?" Or maybe you're one who isn't so concerned about changing the world quite yet; you barely got yourself out of bed this morning. Either way, it's likely that more is in store for you than the life you're living today.

If you want to be distinguishable from the world in which you live, if you want to know *true* worship—elevating, uplifting, God-honoring worship that is unencumbered by your sin, if you want to be a light in your corner of the world, if you desire a new beginning, the kind of power that makes everything strong and clear once more, a good, swift spiritual reboot, then it's time to power up. God's promise of power is not just for someone else— it is for *you*. Believe that God really can (and will) fill you with great power. Believe that he can and will use you to accomplish uncommon things. And then ask him to invade your personality and to grow your faith.

You'll be a better man or a better woman because of it. You will begin to obey God's commandments rather than living in rebellion. You'll have the power to do it! You'll start winning life's battles. The struggles that you are facing in your home, in your family, in your marriage will still be there, but you will have the spiritual power to deal with them. You'll have all that you need to live a godly life and to build Christlike character in you. You will experience the fruit of the Spirit. Do you know what it feels like to have patience or joy ooze right out of you? You stand there, knowing for sure it's not you who's conjuring up that thing. It must be God! And in that moment you realize that divine transformation indeed is running its course.

31

This is what spiritual engagement is all about. It's a daring, vital faith in Christ. It's the fullest work of God's Spirit in the human life. And it is yours for the asking.

Do you believe that you are destined for great, God-ordained things in your future? What is the primary emotion you feel as you consider the prospect of God accomplishing great things through you?

We need to get fired up again, my friend. We need revival. Many Christians have been to the cross for pardon, but they've never been to Pentecost for power. We don't need another historical Pentecost, but do we ever need the revival that took place in the hearts of those gathered that day. And God is looking for any man, any woman, who is responsive to him and responsive to his Spirit, to accomplish great things in and through that person. Second Chronicles 16:9 says it this way: "The eyes of the LORD run to and fro throughout the whole earth, to give strong support to those whose heart is blameless toward him." It's an all-out search—a search for you and for me.

Oliver Cromwell, the seventeenth-century leader of England, was once concerned about a lack of silver coinage in his country. He commissioned a group of soldiers to scour the countryside in search of silver they could use to make additional coins. The soldiers returned from their trek and informed Cromwell that the only silver to be found was in the statues of the saints standing in the country's many cathedrals. "Good!" Cromwell said with a wry smile. "Go melt those saints and get them in circulation!"[3]

It's my deepest wish for you and me both that because of the Spirit's all-consuming, all-powerful fire we'll be melted into the image of Christ, *fully and completely* engaged, and that we'll be put into circulation for him.

2

A Profile of Powered-Up Living

The Hero's Welcome We'll One Day Receive

A few weeks ago, I was on the same flight as a dozen soldiers who were returning home from their recent military tour in Iraq. Still clad in desert fatigues, they also wore the look of unwavering confidence mixed with the general weariness that shows up on the heels of a tough fight. They took their seats in coach, and once everyone had boarded, the pilot's voice could be heard over the plane's intercom. "Ladies and gentlemen, you probably already noticed that we're in the company of greatness," he began.

He went on to tell us the tough demands those men and women had overcome and the various locations where they'd served, but before he could finish his remarks, the rest of us had risen to our feet to applaud the ones who had been selflessly defending our freedom. First-class occupants waved them to the front of the cabin, insisting that they take those seats instead, and with shy grins and a hint of awkwardness, the soldiers stood up, pulled down their duffels from the overhead compartments, and made their way past the bulkhead as good-natured passengers on nearly every row slapped their backs and offered sincere praise. "Thank you for your sacrifice!" "You have served so well." "Welcome home, hero!"

As I watched the whole scene unfold, I couldn't help but think how good it must feel to be given a hero's welcome. Even the humblest people on the planet want to serve in such a way that the ones they serve are compelled to rise up and joyfully acknowledge their service. This is the point of the Christian life, in fact—that we would live out our powered-up faith *so effectively* that one day we'll get a hero's welcome in heaven. One day we want to hear the One we serve say to us, "Well done, my good and faithful servants! Well done."[1]

The pages of Scripture profile a hero whose life ended precisely this way. In Acts 6 we are introduced to a man named Stephen, and before you get any further in this book, I want to highlight the four key qualities that qualified him for that hero's welcome in heaven, with hopes that you and I will incorporate those traits into our own lives and experience a Stephen-like joy on the day we also meet our Maker.

A Character-Filled Heart

The first aspect of Stephen's life that is worth celebrating—and emulating—is that he possessed a heart *full* of godly character.

My friend Mike Huckabee wrote a great book titled *Character Is the Issue: How People with Integrity Can Revolutionize America*. The central premise is that a *single* individual who lives life from a place of godly character can make a *world* of difference. It's true today, and it was true in Stephen's day too.

Acts 6 explains that more than two thousand years ago, the newly formed Christian church was growing by leaps and bounds. In those days, "the word of God continued to increase," verse 7 says, "and the number of disciples multiplied greatly." According to scholars' estimations, people had been added to the church in groups of twenty or thirty a day. But now, rather than God *adding* to their number, he was *multiplying* it. Twenty was now two *hundred*; thirty turned into three *thousand*.

But although the church was growing and thriving, it was far from perfect. Dissension began to rise over the fact that food and other resources were not being distributed fairly or quickly enough to the people. If the church hoped to care for the masses of men and women coming to faith in Christ, it needed to organize itself . . . and fast.

The primary leaders of the church, the "apostles," were undoubtedly concerned about how to solve their infrastructure problem but were so tied up with their praying and preaching responsibilities that they decided their only hope was to enlist a few assistants. These new recruits—"deacons," they'd be called[2]— were to be men of "good repute, full of the Spirit and of wisdom," according to Acts 6:3, so they could faithfully serve as servants who would take care of the physical ministry of the church.

Although there were thousands of qualified men to choose from, the first pick in the church's initial diaconate draft was Stephen, a man whose heart was undeniably marked by godly character.

Acts 6:8 describes Stephen's character by saying that he was a man "full of grace and power." I love the tension of those two words *grace* and *power*. In this context, "grace" indicates godly winsomeness or a magnetizing joy that comes only from frequent time spent in the presence of the Grace-Giver himself, God. In the same sense, "power" suggests not *abusive* power but *submissive* power, power that yields to God's better judgment instead of relying on one's own. The masterful balance of these two traits was achieved in Stephen's life, which formed in him *unassailable* character.

First, regarding the presence of power, in the latter part of Acts 6:8, we learn that shortly after Stephen had been selected to serve as a deacon, he began performing "great wonders and signs among

35

the people." We don't know the exact kind of miracles that were taking place, but it's safe to assume that special power had been given to Stephen so that, just like Jesus, he could touch people right at their point of need. Maybe it took the form of healing power or prophesying power or the power to marshall resources that would meet practical needs. Whatever it was, as a result of seeing the Holy Spirit authenticated by relevant, supernatural activity, people's faith was being awakened, and their lives were being transformed. But not everybody was thrilled with this turn of events.

Acts 6:9–11 says that "some of those who belonged to the synagogue of the Freedmen (as it was called), and of the Cyrenians, and of the Alexandrians, and of those from Cilicia and Asia, rose up and disputed with Stephen. But they could not withstand the wisdom and the spirit with which he was speaking. They secretly instigated men who said, 'We have heard him speak blasphemous words against Moses and God.'"

Of course, Stephen wasn't insulting or blaspheming Moses *or* God, but his accusers knew that spreading lies was a quick and easy way to shut up the man who was preaching the good news. Or so they thought. When their brilliant approach failed, they pursued a more drastic course of action. Verse 12 says, "And they stirred up the people and the elders and the scribes, and they came upon him and seized him and brought him before the council."

Our deacon-friend Stephen was essentially thrown under the bus.

At the infamous council meeting, Stephen had to suffer through testimony after testimony from a parade of people who had been recruited for the sole purpose of lying about him. "This man never ceases to speak words against this holy place and the law," one recruit said, "for we have heard him say that this Jesus of Nazareth will destroy this place and will change the customs that Moses delivered to us" (vv. 13–14).

Person after person accused Stephen of everything under the sun, but in the end it amounted to nothing but a pile of lies.

A lesser man would have sunk to the level of his accusers and sought retaliation, but not Stephen. Because he was enabled by the power of God, Stephen stood his ground and showed sweet strength instead. *He was full* of power and *full* of grace—godly character in its purest form.

POWER POINT

> Think about the last time you were unjustly accused of wrong-doing.
>
> Are you more prone to seek retaliation or to simply suck it up and go about your business as planned? What are a few of the benefits that might accompany the choice to remain calm in the face of indictment?

The result of Stephen's tempered reaction to false accusations being made against him was nothing short of miraculous. "Gazing at him," Acts 6:15 says of the men who had tried to take the deacon down, "all who sat in the council saw that his face was like the face of an angel." Which brings me to my second point: real heroes look a lot like Christ.

The Face of an Angel

When we are powered up by the Spirit of God, the joy of his presence ought to be reflected in our countenance. In other words, if you're full of Jesus, the peace and joy of Jesus should show up on your face. Even better than Botox® is the *divine* face-lift that takes place when God alters a human heart. Outer beauty becomes a reflection of the inner beauty being cultivated by Christ, and it's magnificent through and through.

When Stephen's angry accusers looked upon his face, they saw "the face of an angel" gazing back at them. Now I've never seen an angel, but we're told in Scripture that the angels stand in the presence of God and therefore reflect something of the *glory* of God. Can you imagine how shocked the vicious council members must have been when, in return for their evil threats, they received nothing short of a taste of the glory of God? Talk about jolting! But Stephen didn't just look like a person who would one day receive a hero's welcome in heaven. He also *acted* like it.

A Wisdom-Drenched Mind

Back in Acts 6:10 we are told that even Stephen's enemies found it impossible to stand up against his wisdom. By way of context, Stephen had gone to one of more than four hundred synagogues, or places of worship, that existed in Jerusalem at the time, in order to reason with the people regarding the things of God. Stephen was an articulate spokesperson and a defender of the faith, but many people in the crowd were suspicious of him. They postured and argued and spat out their contempt, but the text says that in the end, they just couldn't resist his *wisdom*.

Imagine finding yourself in Stephen's shoes. You are called upon to give a defense of your faith, and it's obvious that things aren't going very well. Your listeners are filled with rage, and you're more than a little tempted to just fold up your tent and head home. But not Stephen. He stood firm and faithful to the words he was speaking, having no idea he'd be asked to pay the *ultimate* price for that faith. All he knew was that he had an opportunity to share the love of Christ with the religious establishment of his day, leaders who were full of religion but empty when it came to their relationship with God. So he seized it. While Stephen's audience didn't care for his message that day, they couldn't deny that his words were full of wisdom.

POWER POINT

When was the last time you felt ostracized because of your beliefs?

How did you handle feeling left out or indicted because of your faith?

Why do you think God allowed the situation to occur?

Wisdom is seeing things from God's perspective. It's the progressive realization of the will of God in your life, and it's something we sorely need today. We need godly wisdom in our relationships. We need it in our careers. We need it in our families. We need it when we face problems and pain and struggles in life. Truly, we need God's wisdom in *every* circumstance of life. "In all of your getting," the Scriptures say, "get wisdom. Because *that's* where the fear of the Lord begins."[3] And because he knew the Word of God and was living in *obedience* to the Word of God, Stephen's life was marked by *extreme* wisdom.

Feet That Stand Firm

What are the marks of a *real* hero? A character-filled heart. The face of an angel. A wisdom-drenched mind. And finally, *feet that stand firm*.

When we choose to follow Christ—to do as Jesus said and deny ourselves and take up our crosses and follow him—there will be resistance. You can be sure of it! There will be hostility, there will be opposition, and for some faithful folks, there will even be persecution. Truly, the life of Jesus is the most challenging life you could possibly live. It's a life that absolutely *demands* courage—courage that only God can impart, courage that enables us to resist the enemy, overcome tests and trials, and be found faithful on the day when we inhale our last breath.

Courage demands a sure-footed stance, and Stephen demonstrated it flawlessly on the other side of the resistance that he faced. Acts 7:51 says that as Stephen concluded his God-honoring message, he delivered an interesting benediction of sorts. "You stiff-necked people, uncircumcised in heart and ears," he said in conclusion. "You always resist the Holy Spirit."

It wasn't exactly the way to win friends and influence people, but you can't say his comment lacked courage.

Stephen knew that it is a *terrible* thing to say no time and again to the work of the Spirit in your life. He knew that it is possible to get *so good* at saying no to God that ultimately it becomes impossible to ever say yes. He knew that in Noah's day there would come a time, according to Genesis 6:3, when God's Spirit would cease striving with humankind. "Now is the time of God's favor, now is the day of salvation."[4] Stephen didn't want even *one* of his listeners to miss out on the grace of God, but for at least a portion of the crowd, his message fell on deaf ears.

After Stephen concluded his talk, his enemies were so wrapped up in their rage that they rose up to kill him. They led him away, threw him into a deep pit, and then proceeded to roll boulders on top of his head. It was brutal, and it was bloody, but still Stephen's care never waned. Acts 7:59–60 tells us that even as he was being stoned, Stephen called out, "Lord Jesus, receive my spirit. . . . Lord, do not hold this sin against them."

Talk about famous last words! This man who was dying was so full of Jesus that he not only *lived* like his Lord, he also *died* like his Lord. Just like Jesus, Stephen's last syllables were a plea for compassion from his Father above toward the godless people who were killing him.

Throughout his life, and even during his death, Stephen took a strong stand for his Lord. I wonder what you and I are doing to follow suit. What are we doing to stand up for the gospel and for Jesus Christ? Too many of us think the Christian life is nothing more than strolling into the sanctuary on Sunday morning and having a seat. But it's far more than that. Walking with Christ requires more than simply sitting down. It also requires standing up.

What are you doing to stand up, to respond to the call of God on your life? Are you standing in the gap for people? How about helping those who are hurting? Do you provide resources for those without food or shelter? What about the addict? What about the orphan and the widow? What about unwed moms in crisis? Are you standing for Christ alongside those who need your help?

Do you stand to support a just cause or a righteous endeavor? Are you willing to stand against what is wrong and stand up for what is right?

When it's time to vote, as a Christian citizen will you vote your values and your principles over politics?

How are we standing? Are we standing for the gospel? Are we supporting missionaries around the world? The question is not how we *feel* about the gospel; the question is, what are we doing to *convey* it? Are we, like Stephen, standing courageously for Christ?

POWER POINT

What stand are you most proud of taking so far in your walk with Christ? What positive things came about as a result of taking it?

If it has been a while since you've taken a stand, I dare you to step out of your comfort zone, move off of the comfortable pew, and get yourself in the gap for God. Stand up for Christ in a culture that is anti-Christ, in a world that has completely rejected him. Stand up to take big risks and to dream great dreams. Stop wondering or worrying about the risks or the repercussions of your stand, about whether you win or whether you lose, and focus only on whether you are pleasing your God.

We need Stephen's courage to overcome temptation. We need courage in order to pray. We need courage to seek out forgiveness. We need courage for facing down death. "Increase my courage, Lord," we should pray. "I'll bear the toil, endure the pain, and fight for your Word." Courage to match personal convictions—Stephen had it, without a doubt.

You say, "But what if I'm not as strong as Stephen? What if I am actually quite weak?" This, my friend, is where the Spirit of God enters the equation. When we power up in him, we receive strength to survive any temptation and courage to match our convictions. In Psalm 16:8 the psalmist said, "I have set the LORD always before me. . . . [therefore] I shall not be moved"

(KJV). The spiritual steadfastness we seek comes only by way of the steadfast Spirit of God.

If you and I could hop in a time machine, head all the way back to first-century Jerusalem, and ask all of Stephen's friends what words come to mind when they think of Stephen, I imagine we'd hear things like,

"Commitment."

"A servant's heart."

"Loving-kindness."

"A steadfast spirit."

P O W E R   P O I N T

Consider three people who know you best. What words would they use to describe you today? Do those words delight you and make you feel proud, or do they dishearten you and make you desire change? What words do you wish were accurate descriptors of you?

How I pray I will always be known for traits like these! I want to be a man just like Stephen, who was full of God and, as a result, full of things like character and courage. Ultimately Stephen lived for an audience of One. He knew that he had nothing to prove, only Someone to please. And it didn't matter if he pleased the world and displeased God. At every turn he chose to please God.

The Donation, Not the Duration

Stephen, a faithful deacon whose name means "the crowned one," did not live a long life. But he certainly lived a full one.

Full of character.

Full of grace.

Full of power.

Full of courage.

Full of *Christ*.

For our lives, too, what matters most is not how *long* we live, but rather how *fully* we live. Modern-day martyr Jim Elliot once wrote in his diary, "I seek not a long life, but a full one, like you, Lord Jesus." I hope it's our prayer, too, that we would focus more on the donation of our lives than on the duration, the depth instead of the length. *That* is a life lived in full.

The story of Stephen, though brief, is an epic tale of one man who emerges ever so quickly upon the stage of history and disappears equally fast. And yet his influence—the impact of his life and legacy—lasts to this day. Through his courageous teaching, his suffering, and ultimately his martyrdom, Stephen was responsible for launching the church into a global missions operation that persists even now.

Can I give you just one more distinction as it relates to emulating the life Stephen chose to live? Amid the blood, the pain, the angry shouts surrounding him, God's man Stephen, the man with the angelic face who was full of the Spirit and full of courage, knew perfect peace as he drew his last breath. He had lived heroically and was now receiving a hero's welcome. As Stephen looked up into heaven upon his death, we're told in Acts 7:56 that he saw Jesus "standing at the right hand of God."

Here's why this is significant: Normally when Jesus is referred to as being at the throne of God, he is *seated* at God's right hand. But now when Stephen looks up into heaven as he is dying, he sees Jesus standing up. In my view, Jesus' posture is significant because in essence he was saying, "Stephen, you stood up for me, and so now I'll stand up for you."

Quoting Jesus, Matthew 10:32 says, "Stand up for me against world opinion and I'll stand up for you before my Father in heaven" (*MSG*). This godly deacon, this layman who unleashed the gospel of Christ upon a broken and needy world, did not die in tragedy but in triumph. Stephen departed this life in sheer victory because he faithfully walked by the Spirit each and every day.

I can only imagine his elation as he received his hero's welcome in heaven, with Jesus having risen to his feet in earnest appreciation of a job well done. "Thank you for your sacrifice," I envision Christ cheering as he slaps Stephen on the back. "You have served so well, good and faithful servant. Welcome home, hero. Welcome home!"

3

Breathing Native Air

Inspiration Straight from the Spirit of God

Yoga is not exactly my thing, but from what I understand, people who practice it experience clearer thinking, calmer nerves, and a deeper sense of relaxation in their major muscle groups. Too bad watching baseball doesn't have the same effect. I'd be as laid back as a mound of spaghetti.

Evidently a big part of yoga involves paying attention to your breathing. While contorting your body into pretzel-like positions, you're also supposed to focus intently on every inhale and exhale. "This is good for you," yoga masters assure us, and based on some recent work done by really smart people in white lab coats, it appears they might be right.

Researchers both in Israel and in the United States (at Southern Methodist University and at the University of Michigan) have completed studies showing that when you learn how to focus on breathing properly, you can dramatically improve your overall quality of life.[1] Their evidence supports the fact that, by contrast, breathing *incorrectly* increases incidences of panic attacks, hyper-ventilation, hypertension, and "chronic pulmonary obstruction"—the inability to get enough air into or out of your lungs.

But enroll these "bad breathers" in a fifteen-minute-a-day training regimen where they learn the tenets of correct breathing, and the whole game changes. Suddenly anxiety dissipates, oxygenated blood levels increase, mobility emerges, and zest for living resumes—all because of paying attention to a practice that had never been attended to before. Amazing!

The studies caught my attention because I think there is an important spiritual parallel to this proper breathing plan. So many Christians I know are suffering from the spiritual equivalent of the physical maladies those researchers observed. They are panicky and tense and getting not *nearly* enough fresh, life-giving air. They are tired—bone-tired—of their family, their friends, and their church. They're especially weary of the rat race, mostly because they have the distinct sense that the rats are winning. Rather than life being characterized by faithfulness and fruitfulness, it is marked by failure, frustration, and ever-increasing indolence.

These bone-tired folks read books like this one about living in the grace and power of the Spirit and absorb chapters like the last one about guys like Stephen who are getting it right, and something in them wilts a little more. *What's wrong with me?* they think. *If the Spirit-filled thing is so great, then why isn't it working for me?* Determined to crack the code on a more satisfying existence, they decide to increase their attendance at church. They resolve to worship more. They vow to pray more. They commit to give more money. And with grim determination they fix their gaze, set their jaw, and prepare to gut it out. "I'm going to live like a *real, Spirit-filled Christian* this week," they insist over and over, "even if it kills me!" And it just about does every time.

That's a far cry from what true powered-up living looks like.

A Lot Like Breathing

The late Dr. Bill Bright, a friend of mine who was the founder of Campus Crusade for Christ and one of the greatest evangelists of the modern era, was once asked to explain what Spirit-filled living is all about. He thought about it for a moment and then landed on this succinct description: "Living in the Spirit is a lot like breathing."

I like his definition because, for a healthy person, breathing is a normal, natural function of the body. You inhale new air and exhale the old. In and out, in and out, in and out—the simple rhythm that miraculously sustains life. "This is how life with the Spirit is supposed to be," Dr. Bright asserted. And I happen to think he was right. When Christ-followers aren't thriving in the abundant life that God intends for them to live, it often comes down to the fact that they haven't learned the proper way to breathe.

Let's say that you're having a really bad day. You're headed home from work, where for ten long hours you felt like a tree surrounded by woodpeckers, and now all you really want is a little peace and ESPN. You walk through the door, and before you can even say hello, your three young children are tugging at your arms, jumping onto your back, and pelting you with so many overlapping questions that your eyes glaze over and your head starts to throb. You feel frustration rise up from your gut, but before you can cut it off at the pass, you lay into your kids, screaming at the top of your lungs, "Pipe down! Get off me! *Now!*"

Silence fills the air as your kids climb down, drop their chins to their little chests, and mope their way into the kitchen, where your wife is staring, dumbfounded, at the dope she calls her husband. But her disappointment is nothing compared to the disappointment you sense from God. His Spirit convicts you and seems to say, "You know, it really grieves me when you talk to your children that way. It's not right, and it's not like you. Certainly it's not like *me*."

You breathe in those words, reclaim your footing in the land of the sane-and-under-control, and breathe out an earnest confession back to him: "Lord, I don't want angry responses to be part of my life. I don't want to be a frustrated father who then just frustrates my family. I want to bring them joy. I want to bring *you* joy. I release my bad attitude and my anger to you. I am so sorry."

After a moment, you take another deep breath. "Lord, take control of my life. Take control of my personality. Take control of my attitude. Spirit of God, live in me and walk with me. I want nothing more than to walk with you."

This is spiritual breathing—inhaling God's presence, exhaling your preoccupations, inhaling God's power—the correct breathing that can radically improve both your quality of life and mine.

Breathe In God's Presence

I played for a coach one time who could reignite my passion in five words flat. "Graham, you gotta *want* it!" he'd bark at me when my spirits were down or my energy was low. He knew what I had not yet learned: I wasn't going to get better as a ballplayer until I truly *desired* development. In the same way, you won't get better at walking with the Spirit until you first genuinely want him around. He won't barge in; he must be invited. But once he is asked to do so, he will fill you up like you've never been filled before.

P O W E R   P O I N T

> Have you ever thought of walking in the Spirit of God as natural and everyday an occurrence as breathing? What experiences or assumptions have shaped your perceptions in this regard?

In Luke 11:11–13 Jesus reminds his disciples that their heavenly Father will answer their request for the Holy Spirit as surely as an earthly father would rightly answer a heartfelt request from his own child. "If your little boy asks for a serving of fish," Jesus said, "do you scare him with a live snake on his plate? If your little girl asks for an egg, do you trick her with a spider? As bad as you are, you wouldn't think of such a thing—you're at least decent to your own children. And don't you think the Father who conceived you in love will give the Holy Spirit when you ask him?" (*MSG*). The questions were rhetorical. Of course we wouldn't trick our own children. Of course we would fulfill their apt requests. And of course our heavenly Father will do the very same.

On another occasion, Jesus went to a big religious parade that the townspeople were hosting. It was full of pomp and circumstance but totally devoid of godliness. In the midst of their empty celebration, Jesus stood up and shouted, "If anyone thirsts, let him come to me and drink. Whoever believes in me, as the Scripture has said, 'Out of his heart will flow rivers of living water.'"[2] The "living water" that Jesus was talking about is the Holy Spirit—the One who floods a human heart with life abundant and hope everlasting. Again he conveys that the Spirit waits with bated breath to impart life—*real* life—to anyone who asks.

In the example of the work-weary father who blew a fuse with his kids, a critical juncture showed up in the split second that followed his verbal explosion: would he berate his kids further, or would he arrest his freefall and submit to God instead? Even the most virtuous Christ-followers foul up. What's key is what happens immediately after the breach occurs.

"It grieves me when you talk to your children that way," the Spirit prompted that frustrated father. "That behavior isn't like you, and it's certainly not like me." In an instant the man was given a divine opportunity to invite God's participation. Fortunately he seized it.

"I know you're here, God. I know you see what I have done. I know you heard those words I said. I invite you to stick around and lead me out of this situation in a way that will honor you." *These* are the thoughts of a submitted lover of God.

God Loves to Give

There are at least three reasons why I believe God so readily imparts his Spirit to any believer who asks. The first is that God loves to give. He loves it! In Ephesians 5:18 the apostle Paul, under the inspiration of God, says, "Be filled with the Spirit." The word "filled" is written in the passive tense, which means that the object (such as you or me) is acted *upon*. So the verse could read, "*You* must be filled *by God* with the Spirit." The filling of the Spirit is not something we do or achieve; it is something we simply receive—from a God who *loves* to give.

God Knows What Is Best

The second reason God loves to impart his Spirit to believers is that he knows what is best for us. That Ephesians exhortation to "be filled" is not merely a suggestion. God doesn't say, "Look, go home, think about this kind of life for a while, and then if you're good with it, come on back and we'll get you all filled up." Hardly! God issues it in the imperative as a command to be obeyed. Why? Because a life lived in the presence of God is the best life there is.

It's important to remember here that what God commands, he enables us to do. As quickly as he instructs us to "be filled with the Spirit," he comes alongside us and says, "Oh, and by the way, I will empower and equip you every step of the way." More on that in a moment.

God Prizes Relationship

Finally, God delights in filling believers with his Spirit because he prizes relationship. The "you" implied in "be filled with the Holy Spirit" means "*all* of you," all believers. The Spirit-filled life is not just for super-saints or the spiritually elite. It is intended for you and for me and for everybody else who knows Jesus Christ as Savior.

In addition to being available to all, the filling is intended to be *continual*. When you were "born again" (John 3:3), you were officially filled with the Spirit. But the Greek command to "be filled" is written in the present active tense, which means the process is supposed to start but not stop. Ever! The reason we need to be filled again and again and again, as God well knows, is that we leak. We get weary and wobbly and are prone to wander away. God says, "Keep coming back to me, and I'll keep you topped off—with strength for the journey and satisfaction for your soul. Trust me to fill you up, and you'll mount up with wings like eagles. You'll run and not be weary. You'll walk and will not faint."[3]

So God expects that we will come to him each day, day by day, and say, "Lord, fill me with your Spirit on this day! Live your life through me; wear me like a suit; do in and through me whatever it is you would like to do. I want nothing to do with living in my own flesh; instead, I want to live in your Spirit." Can you imagine how much joy a prayer like this must bring God, the inventor and by far the greatest lover of relationships the world will ever know? It brings him *great joy*, I assure you.

Constantly, obediently, and with a glad receiver's heart, let God's Spirit wash over you afresh. Become a person who craves God's presence like you crave fresh air. "To *that* person," God says, "I will gladly give my Spirit. Guaranteed."

Breathe Out Your Sin

So, the first aspect of proper spiritual breathing is to invite the presence of God. He wants to come in. He's willing to come in. But he first must be sure that he can. God can't exist in the presence of ungodliness, and so the next aspect—breathing out—that must occur if we want to walk in his ways is to abandon our attachment to our suffocating sin.

I've long believed that the reason so many Christ-followers are weary is because they are at war with themselves. It's a war between the Spirit and our flesh, and the constancy and intensity of such a battle can create sheer exhaustion in spiritual warriors. They find themselves in the thick of the fight—struggling, straining, and crying out vows to do better—but never seeming to progress against the enemy of their souls. If you relate, then take heart: the greatest Christian who ever lived fought the same battle you are fighting.

⏻

The apostle Paul once was known as Saul of Tarsus, a murderer who gleefully slaughtered Christians for a living. But God had something special in store for Saul. And on the heels of a dramatic Damascus Road encounter with the living Messiah, Saul became Paul, foe became friend, and murderer became missionary for the cause of Jesus Christ.

Paul explains in Romans 7 that even after he surrendered his life to Christ, however, he still struggled from time to time. "For what I am doing," he says in Romans 7:15–17, "I do not understand. For what I will to do, that I do not practice; but what I hate, that I do. If, then, I do what I will not to do, I agree with the law that it is good. But now, it is no longer I who do it, but sin that dwells in me" (NKJV).

In essence, Paul is saying that the very things

  he wants to do

    needs to do

      ought to do

        must, in fact, do,

  those are the things that he does not do.

What's more, the things that he doesn't want to do, he does. Talk about frustrating! As if throwing up his hands in utter disbelief at this do-and-don't-do dynamic, Paul caps off the passage with these words: "Wretched man that I am!" (v. 24).

POWER POINT

> Reflect on a time when you did something you did not wish to do. What are the primary emotions you feel welling up inside you when you think on that particular sin? What does Psalm 103:12 say that God does with our sin? Does his posture toward your sin change your own posture toward it?

52

Have you ever felt the way Paul felt? You know who you want to be but live out the exact opposite profile. You know what you don't want to do while proceeding to do those very things. It's maddening! But the mere acknowledgment of our sinful state is a start. We are fallen through and through, but admitting the reality is a necessary first step in getting what's wrong made right.

In Romans 8, just one chapter after Paul's I-do-the-things-I-don't-want-to-do rant, he says, "There is therefore now no condemnation for those who are in Christ Jesus. For the law of the Spirit of life has set you free in Christ Jesus from the law of sin and death" (vv. 1–2). Paul's words tell us something important about where the hope for what ails us is found—in and through the Spirit alone, God's power in the life of every believer.

Breathe In God's Power

There's a third aspect to proper spiritual breathing. First, we breathe in God's presence. Then we breathe out our sin, which is anything that takes our eyes off of Jesus. Finally, we *breathe in God's power*.

In May 2008 a treacherous cyclone spun across the coast of the South Asian country of Myanmar. As of this writing, more than one hundred and thirty thousand people have been declared dead, and more than two million are homeless and in desperate need of aid.[4] Immediately after the storm hit, United Nations officials were anxious to send in disaster relief experts to assess the damage so help could be provided, but the country's ruling powers denied them entry.[5]

Sounds crazy, doesn't it? The survivors knew they were in dire straits and desperately needed practical aid in the form of clean drinking water, mosquito nets, and cooking kits. Well-intentioned people with plentiful resources and willing spirits begged to cross the border and lend a helping hand. But the authorities of the battered country said, "Thanks, but no thanks."

We shake our heads in disbelief at stories like this one, until we reflect on how destructively independent we also tend to be.

We know our hopeless condition. We desperately crave relief. And yet we tend to deny God entry at every turn.

When I counsel spiritually bloodied, battered, bone-tired people who are trying to pick themselves up from the battle field we know as life, I can give my advice in two syllables: "Just *breathe*." Breathe in God's presence, the native air you were given upon being born again, and breathe out your sin—the wayward thinking, errant actions, and insistence on independence that levels a person flat. But don't stop there! Take one more inhale as you *breathe in God's power*.

"I want God to do more in my life and through my life," you say. "I want to see greater works of his power. I want to be a better husband or a better wife, a better parent. I want to be more effective in my witness. I want to be stronger in my faith. I want to expand my lung capacity by engaging in the kind of breathing that will bring glory to God." Just as the weary father in our illustration experienced, as soon as we are willing to release our grip on sin, space is carved out for us to crave the things of God. Scripture encourages this theme of abandoning old ways and adopting the new, as evidenced by the ubiquitous exhortations to live like Christ.

First Thessalonians 5:13–15 gives a series of clear commands for the Christian. "Get along among yourselves," the list begins, "each of you doing your part. Gently encourage the stragglers, and reach out for the exhausted, pulling them to their feet. Be patient with each person, attentive to individual needs. And be careful that when you get on each other's nerves you don't snap at each other. Look for the best in each other, and always do your best to bring it out" (*MSG*).

Later in that chapter we're instructed to rejoice always, to pray without ceasing, and to give thanks in everything because this is the will of God for us. Then we're told: "Do not quench the Spirit. Do not despise prophecies, but test everything; hold fast what is good. Abstain from every form of evil."

We read these exhortations and with labored breathing th "Lord, I'm trying! But it's all so *much!*"

Then, just in time, we are reminded of *how* we are to accomplish these marvelous things. "Now may the God of peace himself sanctify you completely," verse 23 says, "and may your whole spirit and soul and body be kept blameless at the coming of our Lord Jesus Christ."

Do you see what this verse is saying? On the heels of Scripture's to-do list, God says, "Oh, and by the way, it's really my *Holy Spirit* who will get it all done."

POWER POINT

Why do you suppose God designed the Christ-following life to be so reliant on and focused on him?

He who tells us what to do is faithful to do it in us, because when God issues a command, God enables us to abide by it.

You have probably seen the TV warnings that say, "Do not try this at home." In my view, there ought to be one of those caveats scrolling across the front of the Christian life. "You can try this at home on your own," it would say, "but you're almost certain to experience failure."

If you try to live the Christian life your own way and in your own strength, the only thing you're guaranteed is weariness, strain, and defeat. On the flip side, if you take Philippians 4:13 at its word, then you "can do everything through him who gives [you] strength" (NIV).

How about one more verse for good measure?

Galatians 2:20 contains a four-word secret strategy for anyone serious about being victorious in the fight. "I am crucified with Christ," it says, "nevertheless I live; yet not I, but Christ liveth in me: and the life which I now live in the flesh I live by the faith of the Son of God, who loved me, and gave himself for me" (KJV).

Did you catch the four words I'm referring to? *Not I, but Christ.* It's not me alone, not you alone, but Jesus living in us,

55

Jesus loving through us, Jesus working on us. "But, Lord," we may say, "surely there is something I can do for *you*?" Alas, the answer is no. We can do *nothing* for God. In our human energy, in our best efforts, on our best day, we cannot live out this thing called the Christian life. We must be empowered by the Spirit. *This* is how we develop wonder-working capability in our lives. *This* is how we thrive. The Spirit is God's chosen instrument for catalyzing joy in worship, effectiveness in service, partnership in prayer, grace during trials, and effectiveness in our witness, which we'll explore further in Chapter 6. Every born-again believer who wants to overcome frustration and failure and fatigue and begin to walk in a powered-up way, therefore, needs only to look to the Holy Spirit of God.

P O W E R   P O I N T

We're made alive by the Spirit.

We're freed up by the Spirit.

We find peace by the Spirit.

We're invited into powered-up living . . . all because of the work of the Spirit of God.

Have you experienced these realities for yourself? If so, what were the circumstances surrounding the occasion(s)? How did you know that it was the Holy Spirit accomplishing these things in and through you?

He who calls you is faithful and will also do it. God will do it. But first we must come to the end of ourselves, admit our emptiness, and let God be God. You can give this a try right now.

First, inhale as you tell God, "I'm a broken and empty vessel in desperate need of your filling."

Then exhale: "I release my attempts to live in my own strength."

56

And finally, inhale again: "I choose to depend on you, my one, true Power Broker."

This, my friend, is the beginning of spiritual breakthrough. We cannot grit our way toward full spiritual engagement. We can only *submit* our way there. When we walk with God one step at a time in the Spirit, breathing in his power, breathing out all that's not, we experience the Christian life in its fullest, most vibrant state. Spiritual breathing is what a triumphant, powered-up Christ-follower does, all the time.

"All the time?" you ask. *All the time.* That is the goal. Because when you are faithful to breathe in and out this way, your overall health will improve, especially with regard to the spiritual realm. And the more you expand your lung capacity for spiritual breathing, the greater your heart will expand for the things of God.

PART TWO

Rules of Engagement

I had the privilege of visiting the U.S. Military Academy at West Point a few months ago and was stopped in my tracks as I read the maxim that guides their corps. "Risk more than others think is safe," it said. "Care more than others think is wise. Dream more than others think is practical. Expect more than others think is possible."

Risk.

Care.

Dream.

Expect.

Those are fitting words not just for Army cadets but for Christ-followers too. When you and I surrender to the indwelling of the Spirit and then *act on the instruction he gives,* we will see our world turned upside-down for God.

Even the earliest believers knew that in order to live a set-apart life they would have to stomach significant *risk* and rely on the power of prayer, they would have to exhibit unwavering *care* toward the whims of the Holy Spirit, they would have to be persistent in *dreaming* of the day when unbelieving friends and family members would bend their knee in surrender to Christ, and that would necessitate a spirit of *expectation* that God would provide every resource necessary to fulfill his Great Commission.

Still today an intimate walk with Christ necessitates complete adherence to these spiritual rules of engagement—divine instruction from our own Commander-in-Chief.

4

Praying with Potency

Faith in More than GPS

About a month ago, a story ran in the *Seattle Post-Intelligencer* about a girls' softball team that had been in a bus accident en route home from their game in Kirkland, Washington.[1] Evidently the driver of that bus had recently mounted an off-the-shelf GPS navigation system on the dashboard, and based on explicit instruction from his new electronic friend, he careened his twelve-foot-high vehicle into a nine-foot-high concrete footbridge, shearing off the top of the bus and surprising twenty-one students and one coach with a several-hour stay at the hospital.

Fortunately everyone was fine—except for the driver, who surely suffered a bit of a bruised ego. According to a reporter who interviewed the driver right after the accident, the GPS device had been positioned to its "bus" setting; so the driver assumed he wouldn't be directed down paths that couldn't accommodate his big load. "What about the blinking lights and the bright yellow sign noting the bridge height?" the reporter evidently asked. "Yeah," the driver in essence explained. "I guess I didn't see those."

You and I would likely agree that the driver put a little too much faith in his GPS device that day, but my guess is his motivations were pure. He probably loved that GPS system for the same reasons that I love mine: I want to be directed to the best route to take. I want to know about a traffic jam ten miles up the road so I can opt for a detour instead. I want to get wherever I'm trying to go, and I want to get there *fast*. And I trust my GPS to get all of those goals met.

It's the same reason we gravitate toward *any* efficiency-promising device. We microwave popcorn, buzz through Starbucks drive-through lines, and shoot people e-mails instead of picking up the phone or (gasp!) visiting them in person, all for the sake of saving a minute, a dollar, or an ounce of precious energy. We do these things to make life more enjoyable. To make it more efficient. To make it more *effective*. (Which is why it's so annoying when the popcorn burns, the drive-through takes longer than if we had parked and walked inside, and the computer crashes right before we hit Send.)

Frustrating though those scenarios are, not all effectiveness-enhancing tools go bust. There is one that promises never to fail. There is one, in fact, that will *never* steer us wrong. Immensely accessible, utterly reliable, able to withstand *all* the tests of time, that tool is *prayer*.

The Constancy of Prayer

Prayer is how we connect with God. It's the way we interact with the One who designed us, built us, gave us life, and helps us make sense of our earthly experience. Prayer is the path to living more enjoyably, more efficiently, more effectively, and more empowered—and thankfully it's available every hour of every day, every year that we're alive.

Early Christians knew the power of this wonderful communication channel. For this reason, not only were they faithful to pray, but they also encouraged *us* to pray. For example, Romans 12:12 (NKJV) says, "Continue steadfastly in prayer." Ephesians 6:18 (KJV) says to "pray always." Colossians 4:2 (NKJV) says we are to "continue earnestly in prayer." First Thessalonians 5:17 says that we are to "pray without ceasing."

We get the sense from these verses that prayer is more than the prelude to something bigger, such as the tacked-on "Oh, and thanks, God, for this food" before diving into the meal. It *is* something bigger. Prayer *is* the meal! And if we take the Scriptures seriously, we will fight to keep lines of communication with God open at all times, all day, every day. In other words, throughout the course of our Christ-following lives, more than pursuing any other devotion, we will devote ourselves to becoming *people of prayer*.

Cause for Prayer

People of prayer not only pray constantly, they pray *comprehensively*. Philippians 4:6 says not to worry about anything but to pray about "everything." That verse always reminds me of the great hymn, "What a Friend We Have in Jesus."

"O what peace we often forfeit," the first verse goes, "O what needless pain we bear, all because we do not carry *everything* to God in prayer."[2] When I think back on my walk with Christ, I see countless occasions when I intentionally disconnected from God. Spiritually speaking, I knowingly drove through a region where there was no cell coverage, and as a result, I paid the price. I forfeited peace. I bore needless pain. *Lots* of needless pain.

POWER POINT

What peace are you forfeiting today? What needless pain are you bearing right now, simply because you haven't allowed God to help shoulder the load?

Sometimes it proves challenging to quiet our minds long enough to even attempt to answer questions like these, but give it a try now. Before you read on, offer up your most earnest answers to God.

Surely you can relate. Let your answers to the Power Point questions stick in your mind as you encounter the following powerful example from the book of Acts of what it looks like to let God in, what it looks like to carry all things to him in prayer.

⏻

During the first century, Peter and John, two apostles who deeply loved God, were sharing their faith throughout Israel with everyone who would sit still long enough to hear the good news. But city officials were worried that they would lose control of their citizens if people kept turning to Christ as their authority instead of relying on human beings to direct their lives. So one day the chief priests and ruling elders seized Peter and John, arrested them, and put them on trial for proclaiming the gospel. The same men who had crucified Christ now threatened the apostles to within an inch of their lives. "Don't *ever* speak in the name of Jesus again!" they hissed. "Cease this resurrection talk or else!"

But after a few days the officials who had captured Peter and John couldn't figure out how to punish them—what do you do to two guys whose worst crime is healing a lame man?—and so they released the apostles with little more than a slap on the wrist.

Once they were free, Peter and John ran home to tell their friends what had happened. They explained how they had been thrown in jail and were told to shut up and how because there was no good reason for keeping them incarcerated, they had been allowed to go home. In response to this news, the text tells us that the company of believers surrounding Peter and John "lifted their voices together to God" (Acts 4:24).

They didn't rally the troops.

They didn't plot out a plan for revenge in defense of their innocent friends.

They didn't even decry the injustice of the situation that Peter and John had faced.

64

They simply stopped what they were doing and *prayed*. ("O what needless pain we bear, all because we do not carry everything to God in prayer," remember?)

Categories of Prayer

I've always found the topics of prayer chosen by that company of friends instructive even for modern-day dilemmas. Acts 4:24–30 records their prayer this way:

> Sovereign Lord, who made the heaven and the earth and the sea and everything in them, who through the mouth of our father David, your servant, said by the Holy Spirit, "Why did the Gentiles rage, and the peoples plot in vain? The kings of the earth set themselves, and the rulers were gathered together, against the Lord and against his Anointed"—for truly in this city there were gathered together against your holy servant Jesus, whom you anointed, both Herod and Pontius Pilate, along with the Gentiles and the peoples of Israel, to do whatever your hand and your plan had predestined to take place. And now, Lord, look upon their threats and grant to your servants to continue to speak your word with all boldness, while you stretch out your hand to heal, and signs and wonders are performed through the name of your holy servant Jesus.

Often I'll talk with new believers who want to learn how to pray, and I'll share with them an acrostic that helps me come before God with a proper attitude. The acrostic is PRAY, which stands for the four key aspects of that Acts 4 prayer. Let's look at each one in turn.

P Is for Praise

The believers began their prayer by addressing God as "Sovereign Lord." The word *Lord* is a word meaning "despot," someone who is an absolute ruler, whether that person rules for good or for ill. When the company of believers called on the name of their God, in essence they said, "You who rule over all, you who made the heavens and the earth and the sky and the sea and every living thing that inhabits them . . ." In other words, before they uttered another syllable, they *praised* God.

It's important to remember that the people praying with Peter and John all had been enduring a season of intense assault. The world didn't value them. The world didn't approve of their cause. And the world was now letting them know what their faith was going to cost them. But this is what praise is all about, turning away from the world, even amid challenging circumstances, and toward the worship of the one true God.

This steering of the will toward the worship of God is the first act of prayer. Before saying anything else in prayer, we too are to cry out, "Lord, I know you are God. No matter what circumstance I face, I acknowledge that it is within your control. I belong to the One who is truly powerful, and before we get any further in this conversation, I praise you for your Godness right now."

Prayer is a joyful experience, but it is also a serious encounter with the King of the universe. When you bow your head to pray, let your first syllables be words of praise and adoration for the One who alone is righteous. "You are lovely, you are holy, you are all that is goodness and grace"—praises such as these establish appropriate reverence on your part, not to mention bring delight to the very heart of God.

R Means Renew

After the believers praised God, they invited renewal by feeding God's Word back to him. God's Word brings perspective. God's Word delivers truth. God's Word catalyzes personal and spiritual renewal as it carves out room in our hearts and minds for the changes he is asking us to make.

"You spoke by the Holy Spirit through the mouth of your servant, our father David," Peter and John's friends prayed in essence. Then, quoting Psalm 2, they said, "Why do the Gentiles [the nations] rage, and the peoples plot in vain? The kings of the earth set themselves, and the rulers were gathered together, against the Lord and against his Anointed."

These believers knew God, they knew his Word, and they knew that the best way to gain understanding about the challenging circumstances they found themselves in, as well as wisdom regarding how to respond to them, was to focus their attention on God's faithfulness throughout the ages.

POWER POINT

What do you think is the effect on the heart of God when he hears his children praying his Word back to him?

I teach members of Prestonwood's congregation that the most effective way to renew their mind is simply to speak God's Word back to him. The enemy puts all sorts of lies into our head, but we can overcome them with the declaration of God's truth. This approach requires that we first *know* God's truth, but therein lies the point. How can we keep our way pure? Psalm 119:9 asks, before answering its own question: "By living according to your word" (NIV). Even today we overcome the temptations and lies of Satan by giving attention to the Word of God. Today our lives still get renewed by knowing and speaking back God's truth.

Before bringing your other requests to God, ask him first to renew your mind, your heart, your habits, your priorities, and your attitudes so that he will be glorified more in your life. Trust "the Spirit of supplication," as your divine prayer partner is referred to in the book of Zechariah, to mold you and shape you, to refresh you and *renew* you into the image of God.

A Stands for Ask

According to John 15:7, you can "ask whatever you wish, and it will be done for you." But the reason this idea of asking falls third instead of first in my PRAY acrostic is because God-honoring requests can be made only from a heart that is surrendered to praise and by a life submitted to renewal. The point of asking in prayer, therefore, is not to unload your Christmas wish list on

God. The point is to discover and then agree with *God's* desires for your life.

In Acts 4:29–30 (NIV) the believers prayed, "Now, Lord, consider their threats and enable your servants to speak your word with great boldness. Stretch out your hand to heal and perform miraculous signs and wonders through the name of your holy servant Jesus." The four-point request was this:

- Consider their threats.
- Give us great boldness.
- Stretch out your hand to heal.
- Perform miraculous signs.

Those believers didn't pray for the tough stuff of life to be removed. They didn't even pray for safety or protection. They simply prayed for God to be God in their situation. They brought their pain, their struggle, their tests, and their trials before the One who could cause all things to come together for good, and they essentially said, "Lord, here is what we're facing. Please rule and reign over our circumstances."

What's more, after asking God to be God, the company of believers didn't just kick back and eat bonbons while they waited for him to act. Far from it! They wanted to play a role in effecting change too, and so they pled, "Enable your servants to speak your word with great boldness."

In other words, "Don't *remove* the injustice of our situation, God. Give us courage to join you in *redeeming* it!" I love that prayer!

POWER POINT

Do you consider yourself bold when it comes to sharing your faith? What are the characteristics of God-glorifying boldness, in your view? Who do you know who is living this out?

Boldness is not brashness or arrogance but rather openness and confidence to speak and act on behalf of God. We'll explore this concept further in Chapter 6, but the lesson for us here is that we must get prayed up before we even *think* about speaking up for God. "Give us boldness!" we must pray, so that when we *do* say a word for God, we'll be speaking with life-giving tongues.

Worshippers at Prestonwood often ask me how they can be praying for me. "Pray that God would give me *boldness*," I always respond. "Pray that I would never deny the gospel, that I would proclaim Christ faithfully, and that I would actually live out the message that I preach." Based on the serendipitous situations I often find myself in, at least a few of them must be taking me up on my request.

When I was returning home from my recent trip to West Point, my hosts arranged a car service to take me to the Newark airport, which was about a ninety-minute drive from the academy. My driver wound up being a man in his early seventies named Strauss, a Russian immigrant whose family had come to the United States. This man was so vivacious and talkative that I could tell within the first five minutes of our drive that my plan for getting some studying done was not going to come to fruition. So, tucking my sermon notes back into my briefcase, I breathed out a silent prayer to God, asking for wisdom on how to engage my newfound friend.

I noticed a string of rosary beads dangling from Strauss's visor that boasted a small bronze cross, and so once all of the pleasantries were exchanged, I asked him about his spiritual beliefs.

Strauss explained that he had been raised in a religious home and had always faithfully attended Mass. After several minutes of ever-deepening conversation, I asked, "Strauss, do you know for certain that if you were to die today, you would go to heaven?"

Most people respond to that question with something like, "Well, I sure *hope* so." But not Strauss. Here was a guy who was very religious and very faithful in his prayers every single day, and yet he looked up at me through his rearview mirror and said, "Oh, sir, I *know* I will not go to heaven."

"Really?" I asked, trying to conceal my astonishment over his declaration that essentially he was bound for hell. "Why is that?"

He said, "Because I killed people in the war." His eyes filled with tears as a heavy-duty load of guilt overtook him. "I fought in Vietnam," he continued. "And I . . . I know that I won't go to heaven because I killed too many people."

Slowly and with as much grace as possible, I began to talk with Strauss about Jesus' work on the cross and about his love and about the fact that because of that love, every sin ever committed could be forgiven and wiped out. I talked to him about the hope of heaven and about God's promise of abundance here on earth. I explained how Christ takes up residence in the heart of *any* person who's willing to receive him and about transformation's mighty work, which ensues immediately at the point of conversion.

A man sitting twenty inches from me was nearing the end of his earthly journey and had no idea that heaven could be his home when his last day dawned. I was sobered by the magnitude of the moment.

When we finally arrived at the Newark airport, I leaned forward and asked, "Strauss, would you like to pray right now to receive Jesus into your heart so that you will know for certain that heaven will be your home when you die?"

With a hitch in his voice, he said, "Sir, I want that more than anything."

That simple black car became a bona fide sanctuary for a few minutes as the Spirit of God moved into Strauss's heart. Afterward I stepped out of the vehicle and walked toward the trunk to retrieve my luggage. "Thank you, sir," Strauss said with a wide grin as he threw a massive man-hug on me. "*Thank* you."

I needed no jet to fly back to Dallas that night. I was doing some soaring of my own because of what God had done, and it could all be traced back to the prayer for boldness that I and others on my behalf had prayed. It really is true: when we're prayed up and attuned to the Spirit's activity all around us, we are capable of netting *huge* gains for the kingdom. Ask for boldness, my friend. It's a noble request that God will meet every time.

Y Reminds Us to Yield

The final aspect of prayer involves our willingness to *yield*.

Many Christians I know are great at the *praise* part of prayer, they're steadily getting better at *renewal*, and they're beginning to see progress with *asking* for things in accordance with God's will, such as boldness and confidence and faith. But the *yielding* part? Somehow this aspect of prayer presents a problem.

POWER POINT

What characteristics might yielding produce in a person's life? What is the most difficult aspect of the yielding process for you?

To yield to God is essentially to say, "Lord, I am your bond-servant, one who willingly and joyfully serves your purposes on the earth." Yielding to God means removing the focus from your circumstances and problems and viewing life from God's vantage point instead. It is the ability to submit yourself to the bigger plan being accomplished in and around your life.

That's precisely what the early believers did when they prayed, "Lord, do whatever your power and will decided should happen before the foundation of the world."[3]

These believers were in full-surrender mode before God. And this much I know: when the Holy Spirit sees an individual or a group of people joyfully yielding their lives spiritually, he comes to that person or that company of believers and fills him or her or them to the brim with supernatural strength and discernment, wisdom and power. But notice how the filling occurs: you don't have to beg God for his Spirit's filling; you simply *yield* your way there.

In response to the believers' requests that day, God moved with great power. Acts 4:31 says that after they had prayed, "the place in which they were gathered together was shaken, and they were all filled with the Holy Spirit and continued to speak the word of God with boldness."

Can you imagine offering a simple prayer before God and getting a physical earthquake in reply? Talk about revival! God moved mightily that day, which is precisely how revival is defined. D. Martyn Lloyd-Jones, a great preacher of Britain, once observed that revival is a "glimpse of God, of the glory of God, passing by. . . . The God who is there in the glory, as it were, comes down and pours out his Spirit, and ascends again, and we look on, and feel, and know that the glory of God is in the midst, and is passing by."[4]

God longs to manifest his power this same way in your life and in mine. He desires that we put our faith in something more effective than GPS. He longs for us to place full faith in *him*.

Three Lessons Learned

Let me highlight three additional lessons we can learn from Peter and John. First, as soon as they had opportunity, they spoke of their tough circumstances to a group of trusted friends. Acts 4:23 says, "When they were released, they went to their friends."

Have Friends to Run To

The Bible translation you use may say that they went to the company of believers or that they went to a gathering, but the actual word here is "friends," their personal fellowship of saints. If the church is to be one thing, it is this: we are to be a family of forever-friends. Perhaps you have experienced what I'm talking about. You've been part of a community of believers who shared a distinct sense that they were closer together in Christ as brothers and sisters and friends of the Bridegroom than they were even to their own blood relatives who didn't yet know Christ.

As this relates to our subject of prayer, there is, of course, a deep and marvelous intimacy cultivated through individual prayer that we should always pursue. But there's also something marvelous about praying *together*. When we read that Peter and John's friends "lifted their voices together" (v. 24), we ought to be refreshed in our understanding of prayer as the connective tissue of Christian community. It's what single-handedly unifies us as saints.

P O W E R   P O I N T

There is something marvelous about praying together.

What is the most meaningful experience you have known in a corporate prayer setting? What made it so significant?

We have two campuses at Prestonwood that are situated many miles apart. But we operate as one church via the fellowship of prayer. We are constantly praying *for* one another and *with* one another, not because it's a fun luxury to indulge, but because it has proven absolutely *necessary* in order for us to thrive in God's calling for our church. I believe the same premise holds true for us as individuals, which is why it is so important for Christ-followers to stay plugged into a local church—friends and family members who know you and love you and are committed to praying for you.

Remember, Peter and John were mighty men, powerful men who did great things for God. But they were not so mighty and powerful that they could afford to forsake the fellowship of godly friends. The same is true for us. When we fall into trouble, as everyone does from time to time, we must know that we have friends to run to who will be faithful to "lift their voices together" on our behalf. What sweet relief is found when surrounded by a company of praying believers!

Have Knees to Fall On

The second lesson we can learn from Peter and John flows straight from the first. These innocent men had just been forced to stand

73

trial before earthly judges—in this case, the court called the San-hedrin—but instead of caving in to their circumstances, they appealed to the One we might call the Supreme Court Justice of Heaven. They allowed a devastating situation to drive them to their knees. And when faced with similarly perilous turns of events, you and I can choose to do the same.

POWER POINT

> If you have never tried praying on your knees, try it now. How might assuming various body postures during times of prayer enrich the experience of communicating with God?

So often it is during the difficult times, the trials that seem intractable, that God brings us to a crisis of faith and woos us toward prayer. Can I give you some advice for when that happens? When you face the battles and struggles in life that are sure to show up, allow yourself to be swayed toward prayer. Fall to your knees.

Maybe you're in the throes of temptation right now. You're a student who is tempted to compromise purity. You're a businessperson who is tempted to compromise integrity. You're a parent who is tempted to compromise consistency. What do you do? How do you pray so that you can resist the enemy and overcome opposition to the core tenets of your faith? This is the relevance of the Acts 4 passage, that we would know how to fight and win wars for God's glory. Pray your way through the challenges you face. There is no greater effectiveness-enhancing tool at your disposal.

Trust Fully in God's Will

Finally, there is a third lesson we can learn from Peter and John: they trusted *fully* in God's will. Don't ever think that if you choose to do the will of God somehow you will miss life's best. Rely on God, and you'll get the best that life has to offer. Guaranteed.

Jesus made a wonderful and yet terrifying statement in John 15:5. "Apart from me," he warned, "you can do nothing." It is terrifying because you and I both know how much energy and time we waste trying to go it alone in life. To think that those efforts are in vain—100 percent in vain—is a sobering thought.

But it's a wonderful statement too.

What a *gift* it is to know that our loving, all-powerful Father stands at the ready to accompany and aid us every step of our journey, if only we'll bring everything to him in prayer.

5

Marching to a Divine Drumbeat

How to Stay in Sync with the Spirit of God

Most of my close friends don't even know this, but I play the drums. Or I should say, I *used* to play the drums and assume that I still could if I ever found myself with sticks in hand. I don't torture my congregation on Sunday mornings by trying to prove this claim, but I did admit to them one weekend during a worship service that their beloved senior pastor was once a Ringo Starr wannabe. That is, if Ringo had been in a marching band.

I played drums for my junior high stage band but decided upon entering high school that I'd aim a little higher. So marching band it was. When I was a sophomore, they handed me a drum, a position in the drum line, and a single word of instruction: "March!"

One uncharacteristically cold night in November that year, the Eastern Hills Highlander Band was marching during halftime in Farrington Field, a well-known football stadium in Fort Worth, Texas. We were all clustered right there on the fifty-yard line, each of us making sure we stayed in step with the bandleader for fear of being the *one* person out there doing his own thing, looking like a fool.

I should mention here that my uniform pants ran a bit big for me that year. In response to my complaints week after week, my mother told me that if I would just cinch those pants up a bit or work some safety pins into the sides, they'd stay up just fine. But I didn't listen. I was a teenage boy. Who had time for sewing projects?

That night at Farrington Field as I was high-stepping up to the fifty-yard line, rolling my shiny drum like a real pro, my pants gave way in the blink of an eye, landing with decisiveness down around my ankles. In front of scores of parents, the student body, both teams' cheerleading squads, and God himself, I stood there with nothing but a thin layer of white Fruit of the Loom cotton and a very large drum separating me from the rest of the watching world. Talk about a wardrobe malfunction of embarrassing proportion.

Recently I had the opportunity to go back to Fort Worth where my home church, Sagamore Hill Baptist Church, was celebrating their move to a new worship facility. Decades ago, many of my present-day ministry friends and I surrendered our lives to Christ and were called into ministry at that church under the mentorship of Pastor Fred Swank, who led Sagamore Hill for forty-four years, and we were all invited to come back for a sweet time of reunion.

Between events that weekend, my friend O. S. Hawkins and I took a drive to the east side of Fort Worth in search of some of our childhood haunts. We finally came to the infamous field— Farrington Field—and all I could think about was how terrible it had been to lose my britches, a once-proud band guy who got totally out of step in front of a snickering crowd of thousands.

It's a terrible thing to fall out of step, no matter what the circumstances. I mean, who wants to be the guy who always loses his way, always makes the wrong turn, always bumps into the wall? (Not to mention, drops his drawers!) *Nobody* wants to be that guy. Especially as it relates to following Christ, we want to be known for sticking to the path, choosing correct turns, and avoiding obstacles and pitfalls and pain.

We know deep down that when we say yes to God, we begin marching to the beat of a different Drummer. We develop ears to hear that divine drumbeat that resonates deep in our soul, that *thump-thump-thump* of the Spirit's direction in our lives, but even for the most seasoned Christians, the question still sometimes surfaces, how do I know *for sure* that I'm marching to God's beat?

- How do we discern God's voice from other voices we hear?
- How do we approach decisions in life with confidence?
- How do we know which way to go?

Staying in sync with the Spirit—it's more than a gut feeling. It's more than mere human intuition. Learning to live in step with the Spirit requires learning to submit to the work and witness of God himself. It means learning to *let God lead*. "For as many as are led by the Spirit of God," Romans 8:14 assures us, "*they* are the sons of God" (KJV, emphasis added).

Children of God Hear from God

In the eighth chapter of Acts, we meet a godly deacon named Philip, who was led by the Spirit of God to leave Samaria, where he was experiencing genuine revival among the people there. The gospel was spreading, and great things were happening, but suddenly God told Philip to leave. Take a look at verses 26–29:

> Now an angel of the Lord said to Philip, "Rise and go toward the south to the road that goes down from Jerusalem to Gaza." This is a desert place. And he rose and went. And there was an Ethiopian,

a eunuch, a court official of Candace, queen of the Ethiopians, who was in charge of all her treasure. He had come to Jerusalem to worship and was returning, seated in his chariot, and he was reading the prophet Isaiah. And the Spirit said to Philip, "Go over and join this chariot."

Despite not knowing exactly why he was being sent out, Philip did as he was told. He left Samaria, he walked toward the desert, and he sought out a court official returning from Jerusalem who evidently wanted to know God and wanted to understand salvation. Clearly this was no ordinary turn of events: God was intervening in one man's life by directing the steps of another. "Go here, do this, say that," God had essentially told Philip. And as a result of the two men's encounter, verse 39 says, the freshly redeemed eunuch "went on his way rejoicing." But there's more.

Christian history tells us that Philip then articulated the gospel in "all the cities from Azotus to Caesarea," causing many people to surrender their lives to Jesus Christ.[1] So much redemption, so much transformation—all because Philip had been marching to a *divine drumbeat* the day that God asked him to make that desert trek.

Children of God Are Led by God

God speaks specifically and directly to his followers even today. And when we choose to listen, and then obey his instruction, we experience life that is lived in sync. Just as you plug in a PDA to your computer in order to synchronize information between the two, we are to plug in to Jesus Christ on a regular basis, abiding in him, as John 15 says, so that we live in constant alignment with his perspective, his priorities, and his passions.

Jesus himself advised us to "Follow me" and to "walk" with him.[2] Which is exactly what it means to be a Christian: we walk with Christ, receiving his wisdom, leaning into his motivation, staying perfectly in step with his stride. This is also what Galatians 5:25 means when it says to "walk by the Spirit" (NIV, "keep in step with the Spirit")—literally, to *stay in sync* with the Holy Spirit of God.

So God has promised to lead us every step of the way, not only in the big, master plans of our lives, but also in the day-to-day decisions that we face. I don't know about you, but I take great comfort in that reality, given how many decisions we now have to make. Like about blue jeans.

You may remember a time when there was only one brand of jeans to buy. You'd head to the store, pick out your size from a stack of folded Levi's, and be done in six minutes flat. But now if you want a pair of jeans, you face half a dozen decisions. Do you want slim-legged or baggy? Boot-cut or relaxed fit? Button-fly or zippered? Dark rinse wash or "destroyed"? (Paying for pants that are already full of holes . . . where's the fun in that?) Truly, there are more blue-jean options available today than a person could possibly need in a lifetime.

And what about television sets? In the not-so-distant past there existed but one type of TV. We called it "black-and-white." These days if you head to a mega-store in search of a new TV, you have to select between flat-panel or projection, plasma or LCD, satellite or cable-ready, and on and on and on.

And then there's the grocery store.

At this writing, an average grocery store offers more than two hundred and eighty different types of cookies, eighty-five brands of juice, ninety-five types of chips, two hundred and thirty varieties of soap, one hundred and twenty different pasta sauces, two hundred and seventy-five types of cereal, and one hundred and seventy-five variations on hot tea.

If you like to brush your teeth (and for your friends' sake I hope that you do), you face myriad choices revolving around options such as fluoride or not, baking soda or not, teeth-whitening or not, and whether the stuff comes in a tube that stands on its own or lies flat.

If you enjoy a little orange juice with your breakfast, you face still more choices. Do you like regular or organic? Calcium-enriched or plain? Frozen or fresh by the gallon? Lots of pulp, some pulp, low pulp, or no pulp? Really now, which kind of OJ would you like?

Decisions, decisions, decisions.

P O W E R   P O I N T

List all of the decisions you made yesterday alone. Have you ever considered that God, by way of his Holy Spirit, has an opinion on every decision you make, both large ones and small?

A newspaper reporter flew to Florida recently to do a story on the current condition of the Florida orange juice market. He was visiting a collection site where they boxed oranges according to the fruit's size and health. The reporter stood by as the foreman sorted oranges, noticing that the man tossed the large oranges into a large hole, the medium-size oranges into another hole, and the bruised ones into yet a third hole. He'd sort them—big hole, little hole, damaged-goods hole—day after day, hour after hour after long, boring hour.

Finally the reporter couldn't contain himself and asked the question that had been on his mind for days. "How do you do this dull and tedious job *every day*?"

The man looked at the reporter and said, "You don't know the half of it! From the time I get here in the morning to the time I leave in the evening, it's nothing but decisions, decisions, decisions!"

What a joy it is to know that God will lead us in every decision we face, no matter how big or how small.

Children of God Relinquish Control to God

According to one survey, a majority of people in America today want more control over the details of their lives, and yet the same percentage also want things simplified. It's the great American paradox: we want more choices and more options, while simultaneously we long for those slower, sweeter days when we didn't have *quite* so many decisions to make.

When we talk about doing the will of God, we're not talking about knowing what kind of jeans to buy, the type of toothpaste we should stick on our brush, or the brand of OJ that will satisfy us the most. When we talk about doing the will of God, rather, we are talking in terms of the deep-seated issues of the heart. We are talking about making choices that lead to greater obedience, greater followership, greater usefulness for God's glory . . . all so we can grow in intimacy with Christ. Whole and holy, increasingly redeemed—this is the goal, not just from a heart standpoint, but from a day-to-day-life standpoint as well.

POWER POINT

"The steps of a good man are established by the LORD, when he delights in his way; though he fall, he shall not be cast headlong, for the LORD upholds his hand."

What does it mean to you to "fall" but "not be cast headlong"? Why is it significant that God upholds his children from ultimate harm?

Staying in sync with the Spirit means training our minds and our wills to make wise decisions, decisions that honor Christ. I love Psalm 37:23–24, which says, "The steps of a man are established by the LORD, when he delights in his way; though he fall, he shall not be cast headlong, for the LORD upholds his hand." God delights in the way of the ones who walk with him, offering up their lives and opening up their hearts to the mystical and miraculous direction from his Spirit.

Lives Offered
When I was fifteen years old, I stood with tears streaming down my face at a youth camp on the Brazos River near Waco, Texas, singing the words, "I take hands off my life. It is no longer mine.

I take hands off my life. Let it be forever Thine. Help me to walk each day, close to Thee. All the heart of me, every part of me, just for Thee."

I meant those words from the bottom of my heart as I sang them back in 1965. But over the years I found that I had the tendency to take back what I said back then. As a result, I have had to sing that song again and again as a reminder before God that I mean those precious words still. Periodically I have to come back to the Lord and beg him once more to "help me walk each day, close to Thee."

"Present your bodies [that is, yourselves] as a living sacrifice," Romans 12:1 says. That's worthy counsel, but it carries with it an interesting dilemma: how do you keep living sacrifices from crawling off the altar? Willingly, joyfully, and *daily*, we must climb back onto the altar, lay down our lives, and say with all sincerity, "Lord, here is my life. I surrender it to you."

You may say, "I gave my life to Christ years ago." But clearly it's not enough to offer our lives to God once. That would be akin to the curmudgeon of a husband who said to his wife, who was complaining that he never said "I love you" anymore, "I told you I loved you the day we got married. If anything changes, I'll let you know."

POWER POINT

How do you respond when you feel distant from God? Based on what you know of God, how do you suppose he wishes his children would respond?

Obviously, a love relationship must be *maintained*. And certainly as it relates to our love relationship with Christ, we must offer our lives up to him each and every day. When you get up each morning, offer your life to Christ. Tell him your life is his. Tell him that although you have no idea what the day will bring, you do know that he is near. Tell him you choose to follow him that day. Tell him you're committed to putting him first. Why is this so key to the Christ-following life? Because the alternative is utterly unbearable!

You have probably experienced what I'm talking about. You take a pass on the "offer up your life to God" thing one day and then wake up the next day feeling a small pang of guilt. You rush into *that* day, neglecting to turn over control of your life to God once again and later that evening feel even worse. Pretty soon you rack up a string of bad days, and by the weekend you just want to crawl into a hole, you feel so far from God. You didn't make that first right decision back on day one to surrender your plans to God, and now you find yourself with a bad habit of submitting to your will instead of to the Spirit's.

Offer up your life continuously—every single day—to the lordship of Jesus Christ. As Proverbs 3:5–6 instructs, "Trust in the LORD with all your heart [continuously], and [continuously] lean not on your own understanding. In all of your ways [continuously] acknowledge Him, and He shall direct your paths" (NKJV). Give God your schedule, my friend, your desires, your preferences, your plans, saying, "Here, *you* tend to this today."

Instead of treating God's plan like a multiple-choice survey, where you say, "Lord, show me what your will is, and then I'll decide if I'll choose that way or not," commit to God that you will follow wherever and however he might lead. Tell him that your life—*and* your heart—are his. And then live as though that's true.

Hearts Opened

Going back to our story in Acts 8, it probably didn't make sense to Philip that he would be asked to leave Samaria when things were moving and shaking and going gangbusters for God. Why on earth would he want to move then? And why to the *desert*, of all places?

Philip did what God called him to do because he expected God to do something marvelous in that new place. Which causes me to wonder, do we expect the same? When we sense a prompting

85

from God to do something or to go somewhere or to choose one option over another when faced with a particular decision, do we also follow immediately, expecting that God will do something *marvelous* in and through our lives in that new place of submission to him?

Maybe a dream of yours has died, and as a result your desire for God has diminished. Your spirit has shut down to what God wants to do in your life, and you can't seem to muster the strength to open up your heart to him one more time. You say, "I've had so many missteps . . . made so many mistakes. I'm out of bounds even now, lying in a spiritual ditch with no idea what to do."

If this is true of you, I want to encourage you with the words of Romans 8:28. "And we know that for those who love God all things work together for good, for those who are called according to his purpose," that beloved verse says. In other words, if you are seeking and desiring to follow and to fulfill the will of God in your life, then God will take your missteps (as well as your proper ones) and set you back or keep you on track.

Let's look at how he gets that task done.

When Jesus promised that his Spirit would come to take up residence in the hearts and lives of his followers, he referred to the Holy Spirit as the *Paraclete*, one who is called alongside, "another Helper" (John 14:16; literally, "Counselor"). Therefore, if you have a decision to make or need to know which course of action to take, if you are a follower of Christ, then you have a *built-in Counselor* who lives right inside your heart. And while he doesn't charge a stiff hourly rate, he *does* ask difficult questions.

A good counselor *always* asks good questions—probing questions, penetrating questions. He or she helps call out of you what's really going on in your mind and in your heart, which is precisely what the Holy Spirit will do. And if you will allow him room to move and a voice to speak, the Spirit of God will lead you toward the best life you could possibly live.

If you have a big decision to make right now—again, I'm not as interested in what brand of toothpaste you buy as I am your decisions regarding your marriage or other key relationships, your career, your financial viability, and the way in which you use your gifts to serve God—then perhaps a divine counseling session is in order. In Chapter 4 we looked at the importance of prayer. Let the following prompts—four "vertical" questions regarding your interaction with God and four "horizontal" ones that deal with your inner-world considerations and your relationships with others—serve as conversation starters for the practice of constant prayer, which yields an intimate connectedness to the Spirit of God.

"Does It Align with My Moral Will?"

Ready for question number one in your divine counseling session? Whenever I have a decision to make, I first think through whether or not my chosen path will lead me toward greater Christlikeness. The words I sense God using—gently, respectfully—are these: "Jack, as you consider the decision you're about to make, would you say your plan aligns with my moral will or not?"

Listen closely as you arbitrate your next key decision, and I bet you'll hear him asking you the same thing.

P O W E R   P O I N T

> Does it seem natural or strange to you to engage in conversational dialogue with God about decisions you presently need to make? What experiences or assumptions feed your perceptions about talking casually with God?

First Thessalonians 4:3 says it is the will of God for us to be sanctified—holy, set apart in body, soul, spirit, mind. God desires that we become pure as a result of relating with him. He wants us to be cleansed, to be redeemed in every possible way, and every choice we make in life either moves us closer to this goal or further away from it. May you and I both choose wisely.

"Is It in Harmony with My Principles and Precepts?"

A second question the Holy Spirit tends to ask is this: "Is what you're about to do in harmony with the commands and truths and principles of my Word?"

God provided bucketfuls of insight when he provided us his Word. He says Scripture is "living" and "active."[3] So when you open your Bible consistently, God will consistently speak direction into your present-day heart and life. My friend, God will *never* lead you to do something that is not affirmed in his Word! The wisest move you can make in life, therefore, is to know and align yourself with God's timeless truth.

"Will It Bring Me Glory?"

Next, the Holy Spirit usually wants to know whether the outcome of your decision will bring God greater glory. In other words, this thing that you're about to do—will it magnify the goodness of Christ? Will it increase God's kingdom-building efforts throughout the earth? First Corinthians 10:31 says, "So, whether you eat or drink, or whatever you do, do *all* to the glory of God" (emphasis added). If I can't attach the name of Jesus to whatever it is I'm about to do, I should not do it.

"Seek first the kingdom of God," Matthew 6:33 says. Seek *his* kingdom first. Seek to do *his* will before you seek to do your own. The goal, remember, is to stay in sync with God, not to ask him to stay in sync with you.

"Does It Aid the Fulfillment of the Two 'Greats'?"

Next, it's helpful to let the Spirit ask, "Does this decision help fulfill the Great Commission and the Great Commandment?"

The Great Commandment, found in Luke 10:27, says to "love the Lord your God with all your heart and with all your soul and with all your strength and with all your mind, and your neighbor as yourself." The Great Commission, which shows up in Matthew 28:19, tells us to "go therefore and make disciples of all nations, baptizing them in the name of the Father and of the Son and of the Holy Spirit."

So let's say that you sense God is leading you to move or to change careers or to give your time or money to a certain ministry. Would the change *help you* or *hinder you* as far as loving God and other people well? Would it *help you* or *hinder you* when it comes to spreading God's good news?

You'll recall that our friend Philip was so committed to pointing people toward faith in God that when the Spirit said, "Go," he went. How I pray the same would be true of me. More than anything else, when the Holy Spirit looks upon my life, I want him to say, "Here's a man whom I know will do what I ask him to do, who cares about people, who loves Jesus and wants to let others know about his grace, and who will respond to my instruction with great joy." Certainly when the Holy Spirit finds someone like that, he rejoices! And then he orchestrates great things on behalf of God's kingdom-building dream.

Now to a series of four "horizontal" considerations.

"Is It Born of a Purely Motivated Heart?"

When I am faced with an important decision, it's critical that I carve out room for the Spirit to ask, "Jack, what is your motivation in this deal?" Is my motivation born of a sincere heart, or am I acting out of something such as self-preservation or egocentrism? What is my *real* motivation?

The Bible speaks in Ephesians 6:6 of "doing the will of God from the heart." That's an interesting phrase to use—"from the heart"—because its implications are inescapable. You and I both know when we're operating that way and when we're not. We know when we're seeking our own best interest and when we're looking out for someone else. We know when we're humbling ourselves in a certain circumstance and when we're preoccupied with our own advancement. We know when we are acting out of greed or gluttony or anger and when we are choosing the way of

Christ instead. We know full well when we are doing the will of God "from the heart," as well as when we are not.

"Has It Been Supported by Godly Counsel?"

This is another question I have found wonderfully useful when faced with a meaningful decision. "Has it been supported by godly counsel?" the Spirit has often whispered to me. Sadly, on far too many occasions I've had to whisper back, "Godly counsel? You wanted me to solicit godly counsel?"

Before you make a weighty decision, find a few faithful folks who will shoot straight with you about what seems to be God's will or not. "In an abundance of counselors there is safety," Proverbs 11:14 declares. So seek out godly men and women who know God's Word (and are known for applying it), who can help guide you in the decision-making process, and who love you deeply in order to learn what they think about the decision you face. Perhaps the person is a pastor or a minister, a parent or a sibling, a colleague or a friend. The relational context isn't as important as the person's integrity as a Christ-follower. Be careful whom you select. But do not neglect the selection of several sage saints.

"Will It Honor Your Current Relationships?"

We live not in isolation but in the context of relationship. Therefore, if I'm going to make a decision, I would be wise to consider how my choice might affect the people I know and love. My immediate family, my kids, my spouse, my closest friends—these associations are so key to me that I simply *must* sort through how my actions and reactions might impact them.

We are not only to love our neighbor well; we are also to show our family and friends great love.

"Does It Prompt You toward True Peace?"

One final question I invite the Spirit to ask deals with my gut-level peace on any given issue. Before I charge ahead with a hard-and-fast decision, I listen for the Holy Spirit's whisper: "Will this course of action prompt you toward true peace?"

90

The word picture I carry with me to help me discern what's true peace and what's not is found in Psalm 23, where David makes the declaration that our God is a God who leads his followers "beside still waters" (v. 2).

Still waters.

Not turbulent, rushing waters, but *still* waters. Calm, gentle, and at ease. You are experiencing God's true peace when your spirit begins to reflect attributes such as these.

Let the Spirit pose tough questions when you stand before the key decisions that life seems to present with uncanny regularity. Give him free rein to charge ahead in exploring the ins and outs of your decision-making process. And then surrender yourself to the penetrating answers you find.

Not a Game of Perfection

There's always been a debate among golfers as to what is the most important shot in golf. Some say it's the tee shot. "You have to hit a long ball down the track in order to play the game effectively," the thinking goes. Surely the tee shot is the most important shot in golf.

Some say, "No, no, no. You drive for show, but you putt for dough. It's the putter action that counts! Your *putt* is the most important shot."

I'm a golfer myself, and in my humble estimation both camps are wrong. Do you want to know what the most important shot in golf is? It's *the next one you hit.*

Golf is not a game of perfection. Even Tiger Woods misses every once in a while. There are sand traps and trees, water hazards and wind gusts, missed shots and shanks. If you play the game, you'll experience a little imperfection from time to time, no question about it. And when that happens, all you can do is focus on the very next shot you will hit.

Life is a lot like golf. Certainly we don't always perfectly execute the will of God. Sometimes we miss the shot, plain and simple. But there's always that next shot. There's always one more chance to hit it straight down the fairway and set yourself up for beautiful success.

I can't tell you how many times God has prompted me to pick up the phone and call someone who has been on my mind. I'll call them, and more times than not they'll say, "I can't believe you called me today! I am going through such and such a dilemma, and your call is a real lifesaver." Or other times when I may say something in a sermon that I didn't plan to say or quote a Scripture that I didn't necessarily intend to quote, inevitably someone walks up to me after a service and says, "Have you been reading my mind? What you said up there is just what I needed to hear!"

Clearly, life on earth is not a game of perfection. But if you and I will commit to staying in step with the Spirit and to making the next right move, he will lead us to do *incredible* things on his behalf.

6

Speaking Wisdom's Words

The Case for Being a Camel Not Stuck in a Zoo

A baby camel once asked his mother, "Mom, why do I have these huge three-toed feet?" To which his mother replied, "Those feet are perfect for helping you stay on top of the soft sand while you are trekking across the barren desert."

The baby camel then asked, "Well, what about these long eyelashes? What are they for?"

The mama camel said, "Son, those long eyelashes help keep sand out of your eyes on long desert trips."

"And what good are our humps?" the baby asked as he craned his neck to see his own back.

"Your hump helps you store water . . . you know, for all those long treks."

The baby camel considered everything his mother had said. "So we have huge, three-toed feet to keep us from sinking in the sand. We have long eyelashes to keep sand out of our eyes. And we have humps to store water so we don't grow thirsty on long treks across the desert. Right, Mom?"

"That's exactly right, son," his mother said with a smile.

"Then, Mom," asked the baby camel, "what are we doing stuck here in this zoo?"

That story always reminds me of the Christians I know who are intentionally crafted for a specific purpose and who are given spiritual resources to go great distances for God by sharing their faith but who find themselves day after day asking, "If I'm so well equipped for vast expanses, why am I stuck in this zoo?"

If you are a Christ-follower, then God has given you (and me) a transformed heart, a regenerated mind, and ever-present access to supernatural boldness so that you will speak wisdom's words to a broken and needy world.

It's time we tell the compelling story that we have been given to share.

Proclaiming the Good News

While it is true that only God can save a human heart, he has chosen us to play a meaningful role in the process of people surrendering themselves to Christ. Five times in the New Testament[1] Jesus himself gave his followers—which includes you, if you have trusted Christ with your life—a great commission to serve as his mouthpieces in sharing the good news. "Go into all the world . . ." he said, which in our vernacular means, "On your way to anywhere—in the normal, daily traffic patterns of your life, as you go about your business, living life and enjoying your days—*share the good news of Christ.*"

And good news it is indeed! The greatest good news the world has ever heard is that because of Christ's sacrifice, God's love and grace are available to anyone who wishes to have it. That Jesus died for our sins, that he rose again from the dead, and that he provides eternal life for all who turn from their sin and place full trust in him—*this* is the news that we get to proclaim!

Now I realize you might be saying "Hey, that's all well and good for you, Pastor Graham. You're a preacher! But as for me sharing the gospel? I don't think so!"

Even the most seasoned Christ-follower can face fear when it comes to sharing his or her faith. According to an article I read recently, fear is basic to the human condition, with the fear of public speaking and the fear of death topping the Most Common Phobias list. Based on the number of Christians who are terrified to talk about God with another living, breathing human being, I'd say fear of evangelism ranks a close third, but given what I've observed in my own life as God has expanded my capacity for evangelism, it's not a fear that we have to indulge.

In Chapter 1 of this book, we took a look at the Day of Pentecost, the day the church was born. On that afternoon, the apostle Simon Peter stood before the congregation and proclaimed the message that Jesus saves. It was the central message then, and it remains the central message now. But equally important to the words spoken that day was the voice that spoke them, because like so many Christians today, Simon Peter was no stranger to fear.

On three separate occasions Peter had denied his Lord and had shrunk back from taking a stand for Christ. But now because he was powered up by the Spirit of God, Peter's fears had been replaced with steadiness and grace as he shared the good news. I think there's a lesson here for us today.

Acts 2:14 tells us, "Peter, standing with the eleven, lifted up his voice and addressed them." No longer shirking his responsibilities, no longer running and hiding in the shadows, the once fearful Peter now stood with authority before the same individuals who had been responsible for putting Jesus to death. "Listen up, everyone! *Listen* to me!" Peter essentially said as cowardice gave way to God-given courage. Far from being an egomaniac, Peter was operating as a man full of the Spirit of God who knew he had a pressing message to share. And so, forsaking his former fear, he lifted his voice and shared the good news.

Let's take a look at exactly what he said.

Explaining the Scriptures

When we left the Day of Pentecost previously, the Holy Spirit had whooshed in like a rushing wind and landed in the form of flames atop the disciples' heads. The result was that the people were bewildered as they heard the disciples' testimonies of God's presence and goodness and grace in the various native tongues. Onlookers were amazed at the babblers' display and joked with each other that those folks must be drunk on cheap wine. Which is where we pick up the story now.

Acts 2:14–21 says that after Peter stood up with confidence, he shouted, "Fellow Jews, all of you who are visiting Jerusalem, listen carefully and get this story straight. These people aren't drunk as some of you suspect. They haven't had time to get drunk—it's only nine o'clock in the morning" (*MSG*).

He then went on to quote from the Old Testament prophet Joel, who had predicted that the very scene they were experiencing would one day take place. "In the Last Days," Peter quoted God (via Joel) as having said, "I will pour out my Spirit on every kind of people: Your sons will prophesy, also your daughters; your young men will see visions, your old men dream dreams. When the time comes, I'll pour out my Spirit on those who serve me, men and women both, and they'll prophesy. I'll set wonders in the sky above and signs on the earth below, blood and fire and billowing smoke, the sun turning black and the moon blood-red, before the Day of the Lord arrives, the Day tremendous and marvelous; and whoever calls out for help to me, God, will be saved" (*MSG*).

Peter didn't hop on a soapbox about the people's errant rush to judgment about the disciples' apparent (but not actual) drunkenness. Instead he offered a simple and meaningful explanation of what was unfolding before their eyes, according to God's never-errant Word. It's a grace-filled response that always makes me wonder, *As I look around my world, what errant judgments are people making whom I know? How can I encourage them with the truth of God's Word today?* More on this idea in a moment.

Exalting the Savior

Next, after Peter explains Scripture, he *exalts the Savior*. He goes on to say in Acts 2:22–24, "Men of Israel, hear these words: Jesus of Nazareth, a man attested to you by God with mighty works and wonders and signs that God did through him in your midst, as you yourselves know—this Jesus, delivered up according to the definite plan and foreknowledge of God, you crucified and killed by the hands of lawless men. God raised him up, loosing the pangs of death, because it was not possible for him to be held by it."

Jesus as Recognizable

Through Peter's brief comments about his Savior, he conveys three key aspects of the truth about Jesus, the first of which is that Jesus is *recognizable*.

The word "attested" in verse 22 means "proven." Jesus is a *proven* Savior, in other words a *demonstrable* Savior, the One he claimed to be. In essence Peter was saying to the crowd gathered that day at Pentecost, "Look, you *know* this story of the Messiah's ministry and death and resurrection. This thing was not done in some dark, secret corner. It was done in public, in full view of thousands of people for a full three years' time." Jesus healed the sick, he touched the leper, and he raised the dead. Time and time again he *changed lives*.

Peter wanted his listeners to understand that *this* is how we know he is King. This is how we know he is Jesus, the promised one. We should want the same for our listeners today. Jesus is the same yesterday, today, and forever, and his miracle-working power remains on display for all the world to see. You and I both can stand with confidence and speak of Jesus' sufficiency to break addictions, to deliver broken hearts and broken marriages, to renew entire lives in the blink of an eye. Jesus alone is the *recognizable* Savior.

Jesus as Rejected

In verse 23 Peter went on to describe Jesus as a *rejected* Savior. "This Jesus . . . you crucified and killed by the hands of lawless men," he said.

Now remember, Peter was speaking to the same crowd that cried out for the crucifixion of Jesus Christ. He wanted them to know that while they indeed were responsible for the Savior's death, Jesus' crucifixion had always been planned by God. The cross was not an accident or an afterthought, a knee-jerk reaction by a nervous deity to an unforeseen set of circumstances. No, God had planned it from the very beginning, as Revelation 13:8 confirms: "the Lamb who was slain . . . before the foundation of the world."

Jesus was not a victim of violent crime. Rather, he voluntarily surrendered his life, explaining in his own words in John 10:18 that "No man takes [my life] from me, but I lay it down of my own accord." In Jesus' willful action we find the greatest love a person can demonstrate. "Greater love has no one than this," John 15:13 says, "that someone lay down his life for his friends."

⏻

I read an article in *USA Today* recently about many of the women and men who have laid down their lives these past few years on behalf of their comrades in Iraq. Tears welled up in my eyes as I learned of brave warriors who had thrown their bodies on top of live grenades to deliver a stranger from imminent death. Can you imagine if the ones whose lives had been spared simply shrugged off the savior's sacrifice? This is the thrust of what Peter was saying to the crowd that day. "Jesus came to die for you," he said in essence. "He came to take the full penalty of death on himself, the live grenade of the judgment you deserved. And in response what did you do? You crucified him!"

Indeed, we all—you and me and everyone who has worn the distinction of being human—nailed Jesus to the cross.

When the film *The Passion of the Christ* was released, I remember reading online that when it came time for the film's writer/co-producer/director Mel Gibson to choose the character who would play the soldier who drove nails into Jesus' limbs, he chose himself. He wanted *his* hands to be the hands that viewers saw driving stakes into the Savior's wrists because he understood what we all must learn—*we* are the ones who deserved harsh judgment. *We* were the ones who faced imminent death. *We* are the ones who crucified Christ. "For *all* have sinned," says Romans 3:23, "and fall short of the glory of God."

P O W E R P O I N T

Mel Gibson chose his own hands to drive nails into the movie version of Christ. What can we do in our daily lives to stay mindful of the fact that our sin cost Christ his life?

And yet despite our sin, Christ died for us. Despite our rejection, he stands ready to save. What a mysterious and extraordinary and unwarranted gift.

Jesus as Reigning King

Peter goes on in Acts 2:32–33 to say, "This Jesus God raised up, and of that we all are witnesses. Being therefore exalted at the right hand of God, and having received from the Father the promise of the Holy Spirit, he has poured out this that you yourselves are seeing and hearing." The grave could not hold Christ. Rejected? Yes. Resigned to death? Not on your life.

This is the message that we proclaim: Jesus is a *recognizable* Savior, attested by the power of changed lives; he is a *rejected* Savior who died on the cross for our sins; and he *reigns* as King today, the One who sits at God's right hand. But that's not all. As you point people toward faith in God, equally important to explaining the Scriptures and exalting the Savior is your willingness to *express your own faith story*.

Express Your Story

I frequently talk to Christ-followers who want to become bolder in sharing their faith. I walk through the example of Peter—how he started with Scripture and then talked explicitly about his Savior and was clear about sharing his own faith story—and how I think that his approach was about as sound as any I've seen. In reply, I usually hear something like, "Well, yeah, Pastor, but Peter . . . he was an *apostle*." (Translation: "Peter hung out with Christ and was a preacher for a church and is even in the Bible. What does his approach have to do with an ordinary Joe like me?")

Peter wasn't always an apostle, I remind my skeptical friends. There was a time when he was just a fisherman, a career man concerned only about his next big catch. He was unlearned and uneducated and unused by God. Until he had an encounter with Christ, that is, which is when the tide of Peter's life *really* began to roll.

Back to Peter's sermon. Acts 2:37–40 says:

> . . . those who were there listening asked Peter and the other apostles, "Brothers! Brothers! So now what do we do?" Peter said, "Change your life. Turn to God and be baptized, each of you, in the name of Jesus Christ, so your sins are forgiven. Receive the gift of the Holy Spirit. The promise is targeted to you and your children, but also to all who are far away—whomever, in fact, our Master God invites." He went on in this vein for a long time, urging them over and over, "Get out while you can; get out of this sick and stupid culture!" (*MSG*).

POWER POINT

If you know nothing more than the fact that your sins have been forgiven and your life has been changed, you are ready to be a witness.

What is your faith story? Consider the last time you shared it and how it was received. What do you suppose happens in the heart of a believer every time his or her faith story gets told?

Now, how do you think Peter knew to exhort his listeners to "change your life [and] turn to God"? Why was he compelled to tell them to "get out of this sick and stupid culture"? Obviously, he himself had escaped the world's ways by coming to faith in Christ, and he wanted nothing more than for those gathered at Pentecost to do the same thing.

My friend, you and I don't need to be a trained Bible scholar or a famous apostle to be an effective witness for Christ. All we need is a *story*—a story of how we escaped the self-centered path we were on to go God's grace-paved way instead. Even brand-new believers can be witnesses for Christ. If you know nothing more than the fact that your sins have been forgiven and your life has been changed because you're now following Christ, you are ready to be a witness.

In fact, it's often in simple, everyday moments of conversation between you and another broken individual when God will use you the most. An ailing family member, a sin-struck coworker, a recently fired neighbor—people will see the care in your countenance and sense the strength in your voice as you explain that you know exactly how hopelessness feels because you once were hopeless too. "I couldn't do this without him," they'll hear you say. "Without Christ, I'd still be hopeless today."

The best way to advance the gospel is for men and women just like us to get out of our seats and into the streets sharing Christ.

Preparing Yourself for Usefulness

In Acts 5:42 we're told that "every day [the apostles] were in the Temple and homes, teaching and preaching Christ Jesus, not letting up for a minute" (*MSG*). What was possible for first-century believers is possible for us too: everyone can witness to someone every single day! This is what it means to be used by God.

As you prepare yourself for usefulness, let me give you three keys I keep in mind as it relates to effective evangelism. The first is quite simple: *be open.*

Be Open

If you had to guess, how many people do you think your life intersects on a daily basis? Think about the family members you see, the neighbors you bump into, your friends, your workout buddies, your colleagues at work, servers at local restaurants—the list goes on and on. But the point is this: on any given day, you likely come across scores of people, some of whom God may intend as divine appointments for you.

POWER POINT

How many people do you think your life intersects on a daily basis? Taking into account your day yesterday, what is the number you arrive at? Choose two or three of the people you saw. What would it mean to have shared Christ with them in various ways? How might an encouraging word or an unexpected kind deed "be Christ" in the life of another person?

The best thing you can do for another person—whether that person is a family member or a friend or someone you have just met—is to point him or her toward faith in Christ. *Every* person has sinned and fallen short of God's standard, remember? *Every* person, therefore, needs the work of Christ in his or her life. I would be willing to bet that God is working on someone in your sphere of influence right this minute. And if you will simply open yourself up to the possibility of being a spokesperson for God in that person's life, miraculous events may unfold in your midst.

One word of encouragement as you look for opportunities to be used of God: *never* forget that you're *never* alone. If you have surrounded yourself with a company of friends who are faithful to pray for you, then you have a constant stream of support flowing your way as you prepare to share your faith. What's more, Hebrews 12:1 assures us that we are forever encircled by a cloud of witnesses who have gone on before us, living for Christ and leaving a legacy worth following.

As if all of that support weren't enough, we also possess the indwelling of the Holy Spirit, the greatest Evangelist ever to live, the one who woos and wills that all would know Christ.

Like the camel in the zoo, my friend, you were built for great things. Open your eyes to see the people God sees. Open your heart to be ready to love them where they are. And prepare your feet to take steps of obedience in going great distances for God, which is where our attention now turns.

Be Obedient

Psalm 37:23 says, "The steps of a man are established by the LORD, when he delights in his way." Isn't that a marvelous truth? When we delight in God's way—when we strive for holiness and righteousness at every turn—God agrees to order and orchestrate and guide and govern our steps. What a relief!

This is why we're told in the Bible that we are to walk in the Spirit, because as we are faithful to do so, as we are faithful to speak words of wisdom to people who desperately need Christ, ordinary days may morph into *extraordinary* spiritual experiences.

When you sense God leading you to interact with someone, follow his lead. He may be asking you to pray a heartfelt prayer, bringing another person's needs before the One who can meet them.

Or maybe God is asking you to engage in a meaningful conversation with a friend or a family member. I want to draw your attention back to an earlier part of this chapter, where we looked at the importance of explaining the Scriptures as you share your faith. I have often found that one of the best ways to engage people in meaningful conversation is to mention a verse or passage of Scripture that has had significant impact on you. You don't need to stand in a pulpit to share God's Word. Conversationally, with joy in your heart, just say something simple like, "I try to read a portion of my Bible every day, and just this morning I came across something I think would bless your day. . . ." Then let the power of God's Word do the rest.

Or perhaps God is prompting you toward a specific act of kindness. Clearly, you don't have to be an overseas missionary to be used by God. You can go across town or even go across the street and have incredible impact on another human being. Rake someone's yard. Mentor a young man who doesn't have a dad around. Serve in a sports program. Make dinner for your new neighbors.

There are all kinds of ways that you can let your light shine and let the Spirit of God use you, and I happen to believe that this is how the kingdom gets built—one powerful prayer, one meaningful conversation, one act of kindness at a time. But it's also how your *personal passion for evangelism* gets built! Because once you grow accustomed to living this way, you'll want more and more and more of this life.

Professional athletes frequently talk about being "in the zone." Emmitt Smith, the great running back formerly with the Dallas Cowboys, once talked about entering this zone. He said that it was as if the playing field were wide-open and his defenders were moving in slow motion as he zoomed by. Everything was smoother and faster in that zone. Everything was *just as it should be*.

There were times when I used to play baseball when I'd be facing down a wild pitch, and the ball coming at me looked like a BB, it was so tiny. It seemed impossible to hit! But then there were days when I was squarely in the zone. My mind and body would converge into an interesting display of unity, and the ball coming down the pipe seemed so large and immensely hittable that I would have sworn it was a cantaloupe. *This* is how it feels to be walking in the Spirit. True, just as I didn't homer every single pitch I hit while in the zone, you and I won't see immediate life-change in our friends or neighbors every time we walk in the Spirit. But everything about the encounter will be different when we choose to let God lead. His job is to convert souls. Our job, quite simply, is to tell him we are open to being used and then to be wonderfully obedient when he prompts us to act.

Be Brief

How about one more reminder, just for grins? When you are doing the work of evangelism, *keep it brief.*

If you have heard me preach, you're likely thinking, "Graham, it takes you forty minutes to deliver a message on a Sunday morning, and now *you're* telling *me* to keep it brief?"

What's more, you might whine, even Simon Peter got his tale told in twenty-two quick verses. But I'll remind you that later on Acts 2 says that Peter used "many other words"[2] to exhort his listeners. I repeat, *many* words! So there!

Actually he and I both would do well to learn to be brief, and so would you. Don't make your listeners tolerate a dump truck full of information when a few well-worded sentences will do.

Producing God-Honoring Results

Now, in order to tell if all these evangelistic efforts we have been talking about are actually producing any fruit, we need to look at the Acts 2 passage one final time.

In verse 37 we are told that on the day when Peter preached, his listeners were "cut to the heart." The Word of God had pierced them right through, penetrating body and soul alike. Before Jesus was arrested and crucified, Simon Peter had raised a sword in the Garden of Gethsemane to defend his Lord. He failed miserably and was rebuked by Christ for his actions. But now he was raising a sword of a different kind. He wielded the sword of the Spirit by speaking the Word of God, and he was met with *supernatural* success.

The crowd who was cut to the heart that day knew their visceral reaction warranted some serious next steps; so they asked Peter what they should do. In response, Peter said, "Repent and be baptized every one of you in the name of Jesus Christ for the forgiveness of your sins, and you will receive the gift of the Holy Spirit" (v. 38).

Three key by-products of effective evangelism are highlighted in this passage by Peter, and the first of them is *repentance*.

Repentance

If you look back on your own faith journey, just before you surrendered your life to Christ you likely experienced what is called *repentance*. Literally, the term means the changing of the mind, the changing of the heart. But figuratively it is a word picture that shows an individual who is walking in one direction but then abruptly turns his back on that direction and begins to walk in a new way.

P O W E R   P O I N T

What type of life did you repent from when you surrendered your self to the lordship of Christ? How might your personal repentance experience help you maintain a spirit of compassion as you witness to unbelievers about the love and transforming power of Jesus Christ?

We are born with our backs toward God, and the first steps we take are taken away from him. We live our own lives, enjoy our own pleasures, and do our own thing. And if we keep it up undeterred, we walk straight into an unbearable judgment—an *eternity* spent walking without God's presence. But if we are prompted toward repentance, if we turn around, face Christ, and walk toward him all of our days, then we begin living a brand-new life. And what joy there is in the path of repentance!

Remission of Sin

After repentance occurs and a person's heart is tender before God, there is *remission of sin*. Jesus said that the Holy Spirit would convict the world of "sin and righteousness and judgment" (John 16:8–11). It stands to reason, then, that after a person yields to Christ, he or she is then willing to ask forgiveness of all sin and then be baptized as a symbol of one's trust in the lordship of Jesus Christ.[3]

Repentance brings us to a posture where we can accept remission of our sin, forgiveness for the ways that we have fallen short of God's standard of perfection. Remission of our sin reminds us that we are *fully* and *completely* forgiven because of the blood of

Jesus Christ, and it undergirds the life of abundance that Jesus promises in John 10:10.

Regeneration of Life

Repentance leads to remission, which leads then to a regenerated life. "And [then, meaning *after* repentance and *after* remission of sin] you will receive the gift of the Holy Spirit," Peter said in Acts 2:38.

The reason this was so enticing to hear in Peter's day is because with the indwelling of the Holy Spirit came peace and newness of life. When God's Spirit comes in, we become the *work* of God, which is always aimed at perfection. The offer is still enticing today because every human being ever to walk planet Earth has been born into the world with a hole that only God's presence can fill. Deep down, we *all* crave to become the children of God.

So there it is, the fruit of evangelism's labor—repentance, the remission of sin, and beautiful, regenerated lives—which in this case, according to Acts 2:41, totaled more than three thousand souls. "How beautiful upon the mountains," Isaiah 52:7 says, "are the feet of him who brings good news, who publishes peace, who brings good news of happiness, who publishes salvation, who says to Zion, 'Your God reigns.'" I can only imagine the beauty that the world saw as a result of those three thousand pairs of freshly redeemed feet! And it all could be traced back to one man who ditched fear in favor of saying a word for God, a man named Peter who spoke God's words of wisdom.

Because of You

Last year more than two thousand people professed faith in Christ as a direct result of the ministry of Prestonwood. I stood in front of our congregation one weekend and after celebrating those new to the faith and honoring our people for serving so selflessly, I said, "As we close our time together, let me ask you who are veteran Christ-followers a rather pointed question. Out of the two thousand souls that were saved last year around here, how many of them came to faith because of you?"

Our congregation knows me well enough to know that I would never put them on a guilt trip. But I refuse to deny them the "joy trip" that awaits every person who names the name of Christ diligently and faithfully speaks up for God.

I know, I know—it's easy to look around us and see success-ful, self-sufficient people abounding. *Maybe they already have a religion*, we think. *Maybe they don't need God.*

But the fact is that *all* people need Jesus, *all* people need to be forgiven, and *all* people are living with the fear of death and the sense of hopelessness unless they have discovered a personal relationship with the One who created them and who loves them. Ultimately God allows *everyone* to come to the end of themselves, and when that moment occurs, we as believers need to be ready to join the Spirit in his powerful redemptive work.

We're told in Scripture that "everyone who calls upon the name of the Lord shall be saved."[4] Everyone! That means that all of the barriers have been broken down and there is no elite status before God. Everyone now has access to the living God, and we can all come into his presence and know him, which is the equivalent of having eternal life. Indeed, Jesus saves! This is the God-conceived, Christ-centered, Spirit-controlled message that we are called to share, every single one of us, every day that we're alive.

PART THREE

By-Products of Being Empowered

My family and I lived in Florida for about a decade on property that boasted scores of beautiful, vibrant fruit trees. Like clockwork each season, on the heels of sunshine and rain, germination and cultivation, infancy and maturity, those trees would give up their bounty in the form of luscious oranges and grapefruit.

I used to take walks through the yard, winding my way in and out of those trees all year long, and interestingly never once did I see a tree grimace, never once did I hear one groan. Those trees simply submitted themselves to what is considered *normal* for a tree—enduring the elements, experiencing time's stages, growing big and strong. And as they surrendered to the life they were intended to live, delicious fruit was naturally born. You probably know where this is going.

When you and I submit to the life we were intended to live, delicious fruit too is born. Galatians 5:22–23 names the fruit of the Spirit:

love and joy and peace,
    patience and kindness and goodness,
        faithfulness and gentleness and self-control—
three clusters of fruit reaped from one expert Gardener.

The goal of the Christian life is to bear much fruit and to draw new followers to the message of Christ. But that fruit cannot be manufactured by a grimaced grunt and groan. It comes only by giving ourselves over—mind, body, heart, and soul—to the Vine whose name is Christ.

7

Mind Matters

Firstfruits of the God-Fueled Life

"We have the mind of Christ."[1]

Those were the words the apostle Paul chose when he wanted to remind the church at Corinth—and us, as a matter of fact—that once we are in Christ, we are invited to share Christ's character, his likeness, and incredibly even his patterns of thought. No longer are we relegated to living life from a partial and fallible vantage point. Now led by the Spirit of God, we see all things anew.

In Parts 1 and 2, we explored the *fulfillment* of the God-fueled life. Now we look to its *fruit*. How do you know when you're powered up by the Spirit of Almighty God? You need look no further than to your life's fruit, according to Colossians 1:10, which says that we "bear fruit in every good work" when we live lives "worthy of the Lord."

There are nine varieties of this God-given fruit, as Galatians 5:22–23 attests, the initial triad of which revolves around mind matters—issues of private faithfulness to the way of Jesus, issues of unconditional love and of unquenchable joy and of beautiful, inexplicable peace.

What's Love Got to Do with It?

A young man fell into a state of sheer panic upon turning thirty because he had not yet found a wife. One weekend, while at a friend's dinner party, a woman he'd never before met made eye contact with him and smiled. Figuring he had nothing to lose, he approached the woman and awkwardly asked the only question he could think to ask: "So, what kind of men do *you* like?"

She laughed and said, "Well, all sorts, I guess. I mean, I've always liked the history and heritage of Native American men. But I've also been rather captivated with men devoted to the Jewish tradition." She then went on to reflect on her most recent relationship—"a wonderful, whirlwind six months with a rough-hewn cowboy-type from Texas"—before reining herself in and making eye contact with the man standing before her once more. "Anyway, I could go on and on," she said with a nervous laugh, "but why don't you tell me about *you*. For starters, what's your name?"

"Geronimo Bernstein," he said with a grin. "But my friends call me Bubba."

The two essential needs of the human heart are *to love* and *to be loved*. We want to give love and know that we won't get hurt. We want to risk love and know that it will be worth the investment. We also want to find love and enjoy it the rest of our lives. And we'll do almost anything we can think of to fill the void that a loveless life would leave. We'll try to drink it full, drug it full, shop it full, and deny it was ever empty to begin with. But the truth is, only God himself can top off our tank.

"What's love got to do with it?" Tina Turner asked in her 1984 chart-topping single. And had Jesus been in the crowd during one of her concerts, she could have received her answer once and for all.

Love, as it turns out, has *everything* to do with it. "Love the Lord your God with all your heart, your mind, your soul and your strength, and love your neighbor as yourself,"[2] Jesus would say to the group of Pharisees who asked him which was the most important law to keep. Life and faith and activity all come down to one simple theme—love. "Don't kill each other, don't steal from each other, and remember to serve with joy," Jesus' other instructions stated in essence. "But if you only get one thing right, make sure to let it be *love*."

Upward Love

"Love the Lord your God with all your heart, your mind, your soul and your strength, and love your neighbor as yourself"—I've always found the order of this "greatest commandment" intriguing. Before we can learn to love our spouses and our jobs and ourselves and even piping-hot pepperoni pizza (is anybody else hungry?), we first must get love right with God. Before there can be outward love or inward love, in other words, there must first be *upward love*.

But what does the love of God look like? How does he love us? How do we love him in return?

We know his is a *patient* love. "Behold, I stand at the door and knock," Revelation 3:20 says of God's posture toward humankind. "If anyone hears my voice and opens the door, I will come in to him and eat with him, and he with me." As well, it seeks our *provision*: "He who did not spare his own Son but gave him up for us all, how will he not also with him graciously give us all things?" Romans 8:32 asks. And then there is the *powerful* aspect of God's love: because of his love, we are imparted his power, his self-control.[3]

Still, while we can work to *describe* God's love, *explaining* it baffled even the apostle Paul. Struggling to land on fitting words to get that task done before a slew of first-century believers, he wound up putting the onus back on them: "I pray that you would know the love of Christ, its breadth and length and height and depth . . . the love of Christ, which passes understanding."[4]

When have you felt most loved by God? How does the feeling compare and contrast to human love you have known?

If you're a Christ-follower today, then you likely remember the first time you experienced exactly what Paul is referring to. For most Christians I talk to, their first exposure to the mutual love-exchange between God and his people came immediately after they received Christ. They remember being overwhelmed by God's acceptance and by his complete forgiveness of their sin. They recall feeling freed up as God gently lifted life's burdens from their shoulders and graciously placed them on his own. For the first time in their lives, they knew a sense of calling or *purpose*—specific direction that had been lacking in their life but now was clearly made plain. In short, they remember feeling loved—uniquely, unequivocally loved. So, for most Christ-followers, it's not that we have never known the dynamic of the love of God. It's that we struggle to keep it in first place as we go about our day-to-day lives.

Jesus Christ was the prime example of what it looks like to live out the love of God in ongoing fashion. When he walked the earth, Jesus made a habit of touching untouchable people, loving unlovable people, carving out time to hang out with immature children, and enfolding even the most estranged outcast in heartfelt community. He would be arrested and beaten and put to death for his radical acts of kindness, but though his captors one day hanged him on a cross, it was *love* that held him there.

114

Guilty of nothing more than love in the first degree and agonizing over the physical and emotional pain he was enduring, Jesus cried out to his Father in heaven, "Father, forgive them, for they know not what they do" (Luke 23:34).

> Father, forgive them.
>> Father, *forgive* them!
>>> Father, forgive them, for they know not what they do.

The ones Jesus was begging his Father to forgive were people just like you, just like me, people still enamored with their sinful state and completely unsure of what to make of this "Messiah." Was he really some sort of king? Had he really come to save? Would sin-scarred people like them truly be forgiven? Surely these were mere myths—nothing more than wishful thoughts that lacked any redemptive substance.

But despite the misunderstandings, Jesus understood in response. Despite the rebuffs, he was firm in his care. Despite the bondage, he freely bore our sin. And it all could be traced back to *love*.

Outward Love

It's that *agape* love—the authentic, unconditional love of Christ the Bible talks about—that we are to pursue, love that is stretched out and sacrificial. In ways both big and small, we are to be kept "there" by love, wherever "there" may be for us or in the life of another person. This is outward love, the love for fellow human beings that flows from the strength of love we share with the Father.

When a soldier signs up for military service, he or she offers a life in sacrifice, even before the first day of training ensues. Soldiers know that in the agreement to serve, they are agreeing to die for another. Jesus said in John 15:13, "Greater love has no one than this, that someone lay down his life for his friends." In this way, once we become Christ-followers, we are offering a life in sacrifice. We are saying to God, "I see the people surrounding

115

me, people you have placed in my path, and I tell you now that however you ask me to serve them, I will serve them with a glad heart."

Now, I realize that it's possible you have not ever been loved this way. It's also possible that you have not loved *others* this way. Based on conversations I've had with thousands of people who are at places all over the spiritual map, I know that the subject of love gets distorted and wrung out of shape. The mere mention of love conjures up all sorts of past wounds and devastations. But the second part of Christ's great commandment still stands: each of us is to "love your neighbor as yourself."[5]

What follows are two suggestions on how to become a better lover. I offer them from the deepest part of my heart as a sojourner who has made my fair share of mistakes when it comes to loving God and other people well. I hope you'll receive them in that spirit.

Pray Your Way toward Better Love

Part of what it means to stay powered up by the Spirit involves the fact that you and I *constantly* complain that we're simply not cut out for loving others well. But everyone is cut out for love. *Everyone*! If you have room to grow in this area, then come to Jesus day by day—or moment by moment, if your situation warrants it—and ask him to make you a more loving person. I assure you, he will do it.

When I look at my own life and see how prone I am toward acting in an unloving way, I am driven to my knees in utter dependence on God's love. When I can't love someone else well, it's usually because I'm not loving God well and I'm not allowing him to love me well. I've distanced myself. I've allowed a slow drift from the greatest Lover of my soul I'll ever know. And as a result, I'm a sorry excuse of a loving man to every single person in my life.

First Corinthians 13 demonstrates what love does and does not do. In contemporary English, here is what it says: "Love never gives up. Love cares more for others than for self. Love doesn't want what it doesn't have. Love doesn't strut, doesn't have a swelled head, doesn't force itself on others, isn't always 'me first,' doesn't fly off the handle, doesn't keep score of the sins of others, doesn't revel when others grovel, takes pleasure in the flowering of truth, puts up with anything, trusts God always, always looks for the best, never looks back, but keeps going to the end" (vv. 4–7, MSG).

That's what love looks like. That's what love tastes like when it's practiced in our lives. When we love people, we believe in them and think the best of them. We love it when they win. We keep no record when they lose. We maintain a humble spirit as we relate with them. We prize their well-being at every turn.

POWER POINT

What type of people do you find easiest to love well? Who are the most difficult? How might Satan use your preferences concerning whom you choose to love well in an attempt to distance you from God?

If you can tell your love tank is running a little low these days, pick one aspect of that 1 Corinthians 13 passage and pray it back to God in the form of a sincere petition. "Help me love so-and-so," you might tell him. "I want to think the best of him. I *want* to want him to win. Please place in my heart the desire for his well-being. Change my attitude here, God. I want to love him like you love him." Talk about a prayer that honors God! Trust him to craft in you the heart and mind of a great lover. And then find a neighbor, a friend, a colleague whom you can work on loving well. Everyone around you could use a dose of Jesus' love. Press forward in your goal of being the one to deliver it.

When You Don't Feel It, "Faith" It

I do quite a bit of counseling with men who are struggling in various areas of their lives, and through the years I have heard one refrain far more than any other. "You know, Pastor," many of these men will say, "I just don't love my wife anymore."

What they're typically fishing for is permission to take a pass on their marriage. But what they hear in reply is not that. "Learn to love her again," I say every time. "If you are a follower of Christ and you have the Spirit of God living inside you, and if there is no good reason for you to abandon your wife and family, then make the decision toward love. Begin acting from a place of love toward your wife right now, immediately, *today* until you 'feel' loving toward her once more."

Colossians 3:14 instructs us to "put on love," which implies it is also possible to take it off. I take this to mean that when we don't *feel* like loving, we have to learn to "faith" our way through. Love is a command that is issued fifty-five times in the New Testament, and by this point in this book, you know my posture on this issue: if you and I are commanded by God to do something, then in his power we will be equipped to actually do it. By way of the Holy Spirit of God working in and through us, we will be empowered to do every single thing God asks us to do.

Love, then, is a choice. I can choose to love my wife, my kids, my neighbor, the guy who just flipped me off on the Interstate . . . or not to love. Love is a choice; love is *not* a feeling.

Let me take this one step further.

Clearly, everybody can love the lovable. It's easy to love people who are being kind to us, who are friends of ours, who look just like us, and who have our best interest at heart. Jesus said that even the tax collectors and the prideful Pharisees do that. "But if you *really* want to prove yourself loving," he essentially said, "then I challenge you to love your enemies."[6]

Some people are very difficult to love. I guarantee you have one or two or ten of them in your life right now. They agitate you. They irritate you. They one-up you. They are altogether unkind. You don't even like to be in the same room as these people, and *these* are the ones Christ is calling you to love?

The answer, of course, is yes.

Nearly 100 percent of the time people behave poorly because they are not being loved well. All we can see is their lack of loving-kindness and their blemishes and their faults. But God sees their hearts. He sees the scars they have endured from a day or a week or a lifetime of not being loved well, and he loves them *right where they are.*

I wonder, what would the world be like if you and I awakened every morning and said to God, "Love someone who needs your love through me today! Live out your love for an unlovely one by loving him or her through me."

Think how your corner of the world would change if you maintained that posture as you interacted with your spouse, your children, your parents, your colleagues, your boss, and yes, even the guy who keeps flipping you off. This is the miracle of God's love in your life and in mine, my friend. His command leads to our choice, which leads to a commitment to *love.*

Don't let the people you know live in loneliness and die in lovelessness when you can do something about it. Let your life overflow with the strength of God's love in you.

Inward Love

The last piece of advice I'll offer on the subject of loving others well touches on the idea of self-love or inward love.

Christian author and speaker John Eldredge once said that how you treat your own heart is how you will treat the hearts of everyone you know.[7] If you believe that you are a wretched and unlovable screwup, then you likely will be less than loving toward others. But if you consider yourself a prized creation of the one true God, then you'll see that same beauty in the people you come across. I think this is exactly as God intended it to be, not so we sink into the quicksand of self-absorption, but so the confidence of Christ can have its way.

How is it possible in your view for God to still love us, even when we feel unlovable to everyone we know, including ourselves?

Maybe you cracked open this book today and you're sitting there all alone reading these words, wondering if anybody cares, wondering even if God himself cares. Please read this carefully: *God cares.*

He knows you. He sees you. And he loves you very much. Whoever you are and whatever you have done, you are loved deeply by God. You—with your failures and fears and tendencies toward sin—*you* are loved by God. You don't have to live lonely, and you don't have to die unloved. You can know the love of God—practically, consistently, viscerally—every day of your life. And you can invest yourself in spreading it to the people he places in your path.

Remember, for very good reason, the first fruit of the Spirit is *love*. In 1 Corinthians 14:1 Paul said that we are to "pursue love." Strenuously, devotedly, with reckless abandon, *chase after love!*

Joy's Journey

There is no more joyous way to live than to live out the loving character of God.

George "Doc" Sweeting, current chancellor of the Moody Bible Institute, has been a friend of mine for many decades. He's in his senior years now, but what was true of him in the early days is still true of him today. You can't hang around Doc without catching a serious case of infectious joy.

For as long as I've known him, he's had a saying that he pulls out whenever it's been awhile since he's seen you last. "Do you still have the joy?" he'll ask with a broad grin.

"Do you still have the joy?" That's a good question for everyone who follows Christ to ask because Galatians 5:22 says that part of the fruit of the Spirit is, in fact, *joy*.

From my vantage point in the pulpit every Sunday morning, I see scores of people who look like they could use a refresher course on the finer points of joy. Or perhaps they're utterly *full* of joy but just forgot to inform their faces of this fact. Either way, I'd like to begin this section on joy by looking to the ultimate Joy-Giver himself, Jesus Christ.

The Journey Called Joy

Some people see God as a cosmic killjoy and Jesus as a pale, sanctimonious religious recluse. But Scripture paints a far different picture. Jesus was invited to parties, he was welcomed at weddings, and he was loved by little children. He was quick to love and quick to laugh. Hebrews 1:9 says that above all of Christ's companions, it was Christ whom God "anointed . . . with the oil of gladness." It was a gladness that translates into images of lighthearted leaping, of pure elation, and I don't know a single soul who wouldn't benefit from an extra spoonful of that.

The Bible contains more than five hundred references to things like joy and pleasure and delight and bliss. The great theological statement of the Westminster Shorter Catechism says that "the chief end of man is to glorify God, and to enjoy him forever." Christ was able to live this out, but is it really possible for us to follow suit? The Bible seems to think the answer is yes.

For the Christ-follower, joy first enters the equation at the moment of salvation. "Rejoice that your names are written in heaven," Luke 10:20 exhorts. There's also to be joy in baptism. Remember the story of Philip and the Ethiopian he led to Christ? Upon being baptized, Acts 8:39 says, the still-wet convert "went on his way rejoicing."

There's also great joy when a man or a woman or a boy or a girl enters into conversation with God through prayer. And even more joy when those prayers get answered!

- The Word of God brings joy.
- Introducing people to faith in Jesus Christ brings joy.
- Seeing lives transformed brings joy.

Even dying can bring joy, because it is then that we enter God's eternal presence in heaven. And "joy," C. S. Lewis once wrote, "is the *serious* business of Heaven."[8]

All of life, it seems, is to be wrapped up in joy. More than any other by-product of Spirit-filled living, joy is the characteristic that magnetizes people to Christ. It is what draws people in and appeals to them at a deep and meaningful level. The laughter, the excitement, the optimism, the celebration—these things stand in stark, God-honoring contrast to the bland and calloused lives people otherwise are relegated to live.

Suffice it to say, if you know Jesus, you can know joy every single day of your life!

The Firmness of Joy

It's easy to access joy on good days. But surely you've noticed how good days don't seem to last. You'll experience an extraordinary moment in life that is so rich and grand and wonderful that you want nothing more than to hold fast to it lest it fade away. But then as quickly as it surfaced, it dissolves, vanishing forever from your sight.

This is why James counseled us in James 1 that we should let troubles provide "an opportunity for great joy."[9] Was he *crazy?* Troubles equating to *joy?* Surely he was out of his mind.

Or maybe not.

James went on to explain the progression that leads from trouble to joy: "When your faith is tested, your endurance has a chance to grow. So let it grow, for when your endurance is fully developed, you will be perfect and complete, needing nothing."[10]

Fully developed.

Perfect and complete.

Needing absolutely nothing.

Is there any greater goal in this life? Perhaps James knew what he was talking about after all.

When I look around at the world today, I see plenty of opportunities for joy. You probably do too. The economy has seen better days. We're presently at war. There is evidence to suggest the family is breaking down at record rates. Social problems like drugs and alcohol abuse and gang activity persist. The air in an atmosphere like this can seep into the human heart, can't it? Like secondhand smoke, it wafts into our lives, silently doing its damage and making it increasingly difficult for us to breathe. Rather than flourishing in the sunny state of joy Christ intends, we wind up living under a dark cloud of despair.

Because of these realities, I've found it useful to keep one verse of Scripture in mind every time I pick up the morning paper. "The joy of the LORD is your strength," says Nehemiah 8:10.

Weakened by news of wars and more wars? *The joy of the Lord is your strength.*

By statistics of teens' drug use? *The joy of the Lord is your strength.*

By the divorce rate among Christ-followers? *The joy of the Lord is your strength.*

By the prevalence of sin in your own life? *The joy of the Lord is your strength.*

POWER POINT

> When have you known the joy of the Lord to provide strength in your life? How does that type of strength relate to the physical realm we usually associate with the word *strength*?

When you walk in the strength of the Lord, there is abounding joy, my friend, regardless of the circumstances that swirl around you. "You now have sorrow," Jesus says in John 16:22, "but I will see you again and your heart will rejoice, and your joy no one will take from you" (NKJV). The world cannot give you joy, and the world cannot take it away. Joy only departs the life of a believer when he or she sins it away.

Remember David, the great King of Israel? David sinned against God in some pretty significant ways. And rather than repenting of his sin and letting God set his feet on a new path, he covered up his wrongdoing and endured a miserable few months.

Things were falling apart for David on all fronts—physically, emotionally, mentally, spiritually. But one day a friend confronted him with his sin. Finally David sought God's forgiveness, God's cleansing, God's redemptive care, but not before walking through a dark and joyless season. In Psalm 51 David cried out to God, "Restore to me the joy of your salvation" (v. 12).

God, the great Joy-Giver, gave David what he had sinned away—the original joy he knew upon saying yes to the Lord. This is where joy is found, in God in the character and person of Jesus Christ. That was true for King David, and it is true for you and me today.

I wonder, where are you finding your joy right now? If your joy is found in your health, one bad test result could level you. If your joy is found in your job, a plateau or reorganization will rob your joy blind. If your joy is found in your family, what happens when the kids move away and start lives of their own? *Real* joy is found only in Jesus, our strength on good days and bad, in high times and low, when spirits soar and when devastation deals a tough blow.

⏻

I received a meaningful letter recently from one of our church's members, Debbie, whose husband, Bret, had died thirty days prior after an agonizing bout with cancer.

Bret was in his early thirties, a husband and father who had been invited by a friend to play softball in our church's sports program. Bret had played baseball in college and loved any semblance of the sport. He wasn't walking with Christ and never attended church, but his passion for the game caused him to accept his friend's offer to come and play ball.

Debbie explained in her letter that while Bret had always been athletic and competitive and prone to having a good time, he'd come home from those Prestonwood softball games a bit perplexed. "I've never been with a group of guys like this," he'd explain to his wife. "After we play ball, we actually hold hands. We pray out loud. I've *never* prayed out loud. And I've certainly never held hands with a bunch of sweaty guys!"

What Bret did not know was that during all of those seemingly innocuous games, God was beginning to soften his heart toward the things of Christ. Eventually several of Bret's teammates invited him to attend a Bible study held on our church campus. There Bret began to hear the Word of God and the gospel message. He learned how he could surrender his life to Christ and begin a brand-new life. And that is exactly what he did. Months later Bret would receive a calling from God to use sports as an avenue for mentoring young boys who were growing up without a dad.

Bret's life bore great fruit during those days as a coach and a mentor. But then the dreaded news was delivered: he had full-blown cancer, and no treatment would be able to keep it at bay forever.

In Debbie's words, "God gave us joy through all of this. I know people don't understand how you can have joy in the midst of trouble, but we did."

One of the last experiences Debbie shared with Bret was a car ride to M.D. Anderson hospital in Houston. A friend had offered to drive the couple to Bret's appointment, and as they began the four-hour trip, Debbie heard the song "I Can Only Imagine" through the car speakers.

"We sang our hearts out in the backseat," Debbie wrote. Bret loved that song and knew that outside of a miracle, very soon he would be entering heaven not just in his imagination but in real life.

Bret did soon leave to be with the Lord, leaving behind three young boys and a grieving but joy-filled wife. "Our joy is in the Lord and in the Lord alone," Debbie said after her husband was gone. "Our families were so concerned about leaving the boys and me down here in Texas by ourselves. But after they saw the love that was shown to us by our church family, they realized we were in good hands. We could not have gotten through all of this if it weren't for the body of Christ—the church, the conduits of God-glorifying joy."

She closed her letter by encouraging us as her church never to get comfortable in a holy huddle because "there are lots more Brets out there, just waiting to play ball."

Bible commentator William Barclay once said, "A gloomy Christian is a contradiction." Certainly that doesn't mean we ignore the tough stuff of life and paste a fake smile on our faces. I have down days like the rest of humankind. But even then, the deep, abiding joy of Christ doesn't dissipate. The firmness of joy *always* wins.

The Fullness of Joy

I'm sure there were many happy times with Jesus and his disciples as they shared their lives together in first-century Jerusalem. But Scripture also reveals that life was sometimes tough. On the very dark night when Jesus was facing the reality of the cross, instead of caving in to the situation, he looked at his disciples and said, "These things I have spoken to you, that my joy may be in you, and that your joy may be full."[11]

This brings me to my final thought as it relates to Christlike joy. It is forever, it stands firm, and it is intended to be *full*.

There's an interesting reminder of this in Romans 14:17: "For the kingdom of God is not a matter of eating and drinking but of righteousness and peace and joy in the Holy Spirit." Our focus, then, is to be on things like righteousness. Things like peace, which we'll look at in the next section. Things like *joy*.

When I see a life that's not topped off with Christ's joy, more times than not, it's because that person is denying Christ entry. He or she is holding something back. He or she is saying, "Here, Jesus, you can have 65 percent of my life . . . go ahead and fill that much up with your joy. But the other 35 percent is mine to tend to. Keep your hands off, okay?"

A constant battle is raging in your life and in mine, a battle for control of our thoughts and our minds and our hearts and our souls. And since God cannot cohabitate with sin, he can only fill with joy those parts of our lives that are pure and blameless.

P O W E R   P O I N T

When you don't feel especially joyful, are you more prone to asking God for more joy or to staying put in your pit? What fears or assumptions might keep a person from asking God for an abundance of joy?

Receive the Gift of Joy

"Ask, and you will receive," Jesus promises in another place in the book of John, "that your joy may be full."[12] Not quarter-joy or half-joy or even 99.9 percent joy, but filled-up, topped-off, *100 percent* joy. This is what Christ intends. And when the King is reigning in your heart, his joy will fly high like a flag in your life.

If you're not enveloped by joy today, stop reading, put this book down, and ask God for more joy. Ask sincerely, ask frequently, ask expectantly. God *loves* to give his children joy.

If you desire a fruitful life, then control must be granted to Christ. *Receive* the gift of joy—the fullness of Christ's joy, the completeness of his joy. *Rehearse* joy's words and actions in your moment-by-moment life. And then *release* it to everyone you meet.

Rehearse Joy's Words and Actions

In addition to asking for more joy, begin the practice of rehearsing joy's words and actions in the course of your everyday life. Read Scripture's rich stories of people who found their joy in Christ. Internalize what they said and what they did that bore fruit in their lives. Psalm 119:111 says, "Your testimonies are my heritage forever, for they are the joy of my heart." Let the testimonies of other faithful lovers of God impart joy to your heart each day.

Release Joy to Others

And then finally, once you are experiencing Christ's joy, don't keep it to yourself. Give it away! Release it into the lives of others so that your testimony too will serve as a God-honoring heritage forever.

The Three
Promises of Peace

This is the life you were created for, my friend, a life filled to the brim with great joy.

The story of Chippy the parakeet made national news several years ago. It seems that Chippy was minding his own business one day, perched peacefully on his little bird swing, when his owner decided to clean out his cage. She removed the attachment from the vacuum cleaner, thrust the pulsating hose through the wrought-iron door, and began sucking up everything that had gathered atop the folds of newspaper that lined Chippy's cage.

Suddenly the telephone rang, and so the woman turned to reach for the handset, not realizing, of course, that the abrupt movement caused the hose to flip upward, right in the direction of poor Chippy. In one fell *swoosh*, the parakeet was sucked right up.

Turning back around and finding a vacant cage sitting before her, Chippy's horrified owner yanked the vacuum cleaner's cord from the wall. She dropped the phone to the floor, immediately disengaged the vacuum bag, unzipped it with jittery hands, and fished through the puffs of dirt and debris until she found her little Chippy, quite covered in dust and grime but thankfully at least still alive.

The woman cupped her hands gently around shocked and stunned Chippy and ran into the bathroom, where the sink was small and clean. She doused her soiled pet with flicks of water, cleaning his feathers inch by inch until Chippy was shivering from beak to toe. Noticing this, the woman plugged in her hair dryer and proceeded to blast the poor bird with hot air.

The local newspaper caught wind of this story and decided to send a reporter to talk to the lady and see how little Chippy was doing. The lady said, "Sadly, Chippy doesn't sing much anymore. Ever since The Incident, he just sort of sits there and stares."

Now, when I first read about Chippy, I thought the story would make the *perfect* illustration for a sermon I was giving on the subject of peace. Chippy's tale was funny, it had universal appeal, and it did a good job of describing metaphorically the mind-blowing events that unfold in life and threaten to rob us of our peace. Until I started experiencing a few Chippy Days myself, that is, which is when I decided it wasn't so cute after all.

Surely you've endured a few Chippy Days too, times when you've been sucked down, washed up, and blown away. The most amazing thing to me is that those days tend to come out of nowhere. You're rolling on, enjoying life and living for God, and then *whammo*, a Chippy Day comes on with full force and knocks your feathers back.

P O W E R   P O I N T

What have a few of your Chippy Days looked like? If God is sovereign over the entire universe, why does he allow Chippy Days into our lives?

A storm rises up. A situation unfolds. A middle-of-the-night phone call brings sad news. An accident happens. A devastating diagnosis is given. Divorce papers are served. What was calm is now chaotic.

What was tranquil now is traumatic. What was unified is now broken apart. But when the dust finally settles and the storm clouds fade, there stands Christ, with perfect peace held in his hands.

For whatever situation you face, for whatever is blowing you away right now, this much I know to be true: Christ stands by to bring you peace. If you will only pursue it, he will be faithful to provide it. Guaranteed.

Pursuing Peace: Look to God's Love

First Peter 5:7 says that we can cast all our cares upon God because he cares for us. Now, I realize that when you read that promise, you may glaze over into Bible-Reading Mode. Bible-Reading Mode causes us to skim profound truth and truncate the abundance that God offers. In case that is the mode you're in today, allow me to deliver that good news again: if you are a follower of Christ, then any hour of any day—or any wee hour of any night—you can cast your cares, your concerns, your worries, your peace-robbers upon God, knowing full well that he cares for you.

Tell him, "This is too much for me to bear, Father. Would you meet me right here in this pain?" Ask him to comfort you, to soothe you, to refresh your belief that his peace is near. Then trust him to reveal aspects of your life that need refinement, areas where you're robbing *yourself* of peace by the choices that you're making and the actions that you're taking.

Pursuing Peace: Honor God's Word

Psalm 119:165 astounds me afresh every time I read it. "Great peace have those who love your law," it promises, "nothing can make them stumble."

POWER POINT

"Great peace have those who love your law. Nothing can make them stumble." In what areas are you most prone to stumbling these days?

I don't know about you, but I have a hard time believing that just because we agree to love God's Law, we'll be safe from every single stumble-worthy thing we come across. But that is in fact what the text says. "Nothing can make them stumble."

Nothing. *Nada*. Zilch. Zero. Zippo. End of discussion.

That's the kind of life I wish to lead!

Look to God's Word, and live from the truth of it. Regardless of what peace-robbers you may face today, you can rest your head on your pillow tonight in perfect peace and sleep more soundly than you ever have before. You can rest your racing heart and your mind that swirls with what-ifs. You can rest your seeking and striving for peace, knowing that it has already been provided in full. Is your blood pressure dropping already?

Pursuing Peace: Lean on God's Grace

Finally, let's agree together that after we look to God's love and honor his Word, we will lean on his grace.

Years ago I memorized the words of Isaiah 26:3, which says, "You keep him in perfect peace whose mind is stayed on you, because he trusts in you." In other words, God will keep us firmly planted in peace as long as we keep our minds firmly planted on him. Why? Because when we're meditating on God and on godliness—when we're "laid out," as the word translated "stayed" means—he can trust us to represent him to the world and to bring him glory at every turn. Certainly it's one thing to *find* peace during one of those dark nights of the soul. But it's quite another to be assured we will be *kept* there. "Stayed upon Jehovah," the song goes, "hearts are fully blessed. Finding, as he promised, perfect peace and rest."[13] What a promise!

Look to God's love. Honor his Word in your life. Lean on his grace. Then the three promises of peace will come to fruition for you, promises for peace of mind, peace at home, and peace on earth.

The Promises of Peace: Peace of Mind

Over the past decade, chances are you've seen a few Southwest Airlines "Want to get away?" commercials. They feature "major mess-ups that make people want to crawl under a rock—but a Southwest fare special provides an enticing alternative."[14] So, for example, the screen pans to a museum curator who is explaining to several visitors the tedious and laborious steps involved in sand painting. Suddenly a woman standing nearby sneezes and destroys his entire creation. The screen dips to black before popping up with Southwest's airplane logo and the words, "Want to get away?"

It's a great premise, if not a little too true of real life.

Sometimes we *do* want to get away. We want to distance ourselves from our goof-ups and upsets and problems and pain and our all-too-needy circle of friends. We want to head to some far-off land where we can smile and laugh and live worry-free. But the problem is this: we can get our bodies away, but as long as our hearts are filled with turmoil, any destination we select will be a place of turmoil as soon as we arrive.

Peace doesn't come by getting away. It comes by way of Christ alone.

Peace of mind is that personal peace that invades our thought patterns and settles us down. In the Old Testament it was called *shalom*—a Hebrew word still used often in the Middle East as a greeting that means "good to you, all the best to you, God's peace to you." *Shalom* is inner wellness or well-being, the *inside presence* of peace in a person's life. Such peace comes from *Jehovah Shalom*—the God of Peace (Judges 6:24, KJV, NLT)—and is sorely needed by us all.

A guy in a little country town, the story goes, decided to hire a professional worrier. Gone were the days of worrying over his rent, his salary, his expenses, his family, the weather, and tomorrow's problems. He would hire someone to carry all of that.

One day he walked into the barbershop to get a quick trim, and the atmosphere surrounding him was suddenly completely different. Everyone in the shop couldn't help but notice—where was the worrying friend they'd all come to know and love? This guy was so calm and peaceful that it was totally unnerving!

Finally, unable to stand it any longer, the barber piped up. "My friend, what happened to you?"

The former worrier said, "Oh, didn't you men hear about the new guy who moved to town? He's a professional worrier. You pay him a fee, and he'll do all your worrying for you. So I hired him."

The barber said, "Really? How much does he cost?"

The man said, "A thousand bucks a day."

The group protested in unison, "Man, you can't afford a thousand bucks a day!"

"Hey, I'm not worried about it," he said. "That's *his* problem."

I assure you, you don't need to run out and hire a professional worrier. If you know Jesus, then you have One who has promised to take all of your cares and all of your worries from you, every moment of every day.

P O W E R   P O I N T

> If you were given a professional worrier free of charge this week,
> what three things would you ask him to worry about for you?

"*Peace* I leave with you," Jesus said as he offered his last words to his disciples before he was put to death on the cross. "My peace I give to you. Not as the world gives do I give to you. Let not your hearts be troubled, neither let them be afraid."[15]

More than being comforting to the disciples that day, this is worthy counsel for you and me now. In my own life, when I get uptight and filled with worry, it's generally because I'm refusing to trust the God who loves me and who wants to shoulder my concerns for me. I insist on carrying my cares myself, gutting it out while I wrestle my issues to the ground, instead of being willing to stop and remind myself that God has a better way.

Mere hours after Jesus granted his followers his peace, he had to take a dose of his own medicine. While on the cross, he had to place full trust in the Father, believing that perfect peace would be his even as he suffered and died. It was an adjustment of his will to the Father's will, the deliberate pursuit of peace. And when we obediently conform our will to God's, the same peace can be ours.

Perhaps you've heard the story of Horatio Spafford, the writer of the great hymn, "It Is Well with My Soul." He had been a successful lawyer and investor, but he lost everything in the Chicago Fire of 1871.

Two years later, needing a break from the hard work of rebuilding their lives, he and his wife scheduled a family vacation to Europe. Work obligations caused Spafford to stay back in Chicago for a few extra days, but he sent his wife and four daughters on ahead. They traveled by ship, but that vessel sank, and all four daughters were lost at sea. When Spafford boarded a ship to go meet his grieving wife, he sailed through the same stretch of ocean that had captured his beloved children.

While staring at those seas, he wrote:

> When peace, like a river, attendeth my way,
> When sorrows like sea billows roll;
> Whatever my lot, Thou hast taught me to say,
> "It is well, it is well, with my soul."

That is *shalom*—personal peace that declares to the God who knows all, who sees all, and who is sovereign over all, "It is well with my soul." The wind and waves may be howling and the rains threaten to take you down, but Jesus says, "My peace I give to you." Let life be well with your soul.

The Promises of Peace: Peace at Home

As part of a survey, a group of husbands was once asked, "What do you want most in your life and in your home and in your family?" Interestingly, the number one vote-getter was peace. "We want peace in our homes," the men said. More than more money, more sex, or a bigger TV, interestingly they picked peace.

I'm sure their wives would have voted the same way had they been polled. And yet there remains so much dissonance and disappointment in people's lives and homes today. There are pressures and stresses and deadlines galore. As a result, we stay agitated and irritated and downright worn-out. It's not that we don't *want* peace. It's just that we're not sure how to go about getting it.

When the apostle Paul describes peace in the New Testament, he uses the word *eirene*, which means "to come together," as when two parties unite. What was once separate is now reconciled. What was fragmented has been made whole. This is the peace God promises, so that in our relational world, in terms of establishing peace in our homes, true unity is a reasonable aim. Remember, back in the book of Isaiah, God said through the prophet that if only his people had heeded his commandments, God's peace in them would have been "like a river, and [their] righteousness like the waves of the sea."[16]

This seems too easy to be true—that if we merely keep God's commandments we'll see a river of peace flow through our lives. But tell me, how peace-filled did you feel the last time you stepped out of bounds from God? The last time you knowingly sinned—you either willingly went your own way instead of deferring to God's best plan for your life or you willfully avoided doing something God was explicitly asking you to do—would the word *peace* characterize the experience for you?

My bet is your answer is no.

POWER POINT

If you're a Christ-follower, you know that to step outside the will of God is sheer misery. To live in peace is to obey God's will, regardless of what the world—and our own seemingly better judgment—says.

I want to leave a visual image in your mind as we wrap up this section on peace at home, an image of the apostle Simon Peter on the day when Christ called him to step out of the boat and walk on the water. Matthew 14 tells the story this way:

> But when the disciples saw him walking on the sea, they were terrified, and said, "It is a ghost!" and they cried out in fear. But immediately Jesus spoke to them, saying, "Take heart; it is I. Do not be afraid." And Peter answered him, "Lord, if it is you, command me to come to you on the water." He said, "Come."
>
> So Peter got out of the boat and walked on the water and came to Jesus. But when he saw the wind, he was afraid, and beginning to sink he cried out, "Lord, save me." Jesus immediately reached out his hand and took hold of him, saying to him, "O you of little faith, why did you doubt?" And when they got into the boat, the wind ceased. And those in the boat worshiped him, saying, "Truly you are the Son of God." (vv. 26–33)

What has always intrigued me about this passage is that as long as Peter kept his eyes on his Lord, he did just fine. The waves broke, and the storms swirled, and yet when he focused on Christ, his steps were steady. But when Peter focused on his circumstances and his own discomfort at doing something as strange as traipsing across the sea, he began to sink.

I challenge you to approach your next relational interaction as though you are Peter stepping out of the boat. As you communicate with your spouse, your child, your boss, or your neighbor, rely solely on Christ to guide your every syllable. Keep your eyes trained on the Savior throughout the entire dialogue, and see if the experience promotes greater unity between you and the other person.

How critically we need to be reminded that in Christ we have become not troublemakers but peacemakers. "*Blessed* are the peacemakers," Jesus says in Matthew 5:9, "for they shall be called sons of God" (emphasis added). May you and I wear the title well, allowing God's perfect peace to flow from us toward everyone we meet.

The Promises of Peace: Peace on Earth

Ready for our final promise of peace? This one deals with establishing peace on earth, something every person I know is anxious to achieve. As you'd guess, just as with peace of mind and peace at home, peace on earth is only possible by way of Jesus.

There is an order to certain words or topics in Scripture that remains the same with each appearance. For example, the Bible always refers to believing and then being baptized. You'll never see the inverse; you'll never read of Christ exhorting us to be baptized and then to believe.

Similarly, Scripture always says to first repent and then to believe.

As it relates to our subject of peace, there is an immutable word order in the Bible that is critical to understand. The Word of God never speaks of peace and then grace but instead always conveys grace and *then* peace. "Grace and peace to you," Paul says in Romans 1:7 (NIV). "Grace to you and peace from God our Father," he says again in Galatians 1:3. "Grace to you and peace," reads 1 Thessalonians 1:1.

The point is this: you and I can never know God's peace until we first know his grace, until we have received the gift and the grace of the Lord Jesus Christ.

I grew up in the 1960s, and my generation shouted for peace. We sang for peace, we protested for peace, and we signaled for it with our rabbit-ear fingers. "Give peace a chance!" we'd cheer, even as we were failing to do so ourselves.

Christ's peace, on the other hand, doesn't require shouting or protesting or hand signals. It needs only *grace*. Because to know God's grace is to usher in his peace. Always.

Jesus himself is known as "the Prince of Peace." Everywhere he went, though he was often harried and hurried by others, he walked in confidence, strength, and steadfastness. Never out of sync with God, he experienced utterly perfect peace.

On one occasion, Jesus fell asleep in the bottom of a boat that was sailing through a massive storm. His crewmates were terrified, but Jesus was at peace. "Peace! Be still!" he proclaimed to the wind and the waves in Mark 4:39. And indeed nature's wrath just fell at his feet.

POWER POINT

What situations in your life do you need Jesus to proclaim, "Peace! Be still!" over? Do you believe that he is capable of calming your storms? What words would you use in asking him to do so now?

When Jesus was accosted by demonic spirits, he remained perfectly at peace, showing no panic, no fear, and no dread. Later, in the Garden of Gethsemane, when he was surrendering his will to do the will of the Father, pouring out drops of blood in preparation for the cross, he still knew all-consuming peace. Jesus' accusers would come to arrest him, insisting he wasn't who he said he was, and Peter defensively drew a sword to declare war. But Jesus was the peacemaker even then. He touched the ear of the centurion who had lost to Peter's sword and restored, renewed, healed.

Peace-Giver.

Peacemaker.

Peace-Seeker.

This is the Jesus we serve.

Even on the cross, with shouted blasphemes and obscenities swirling around him, Jesus was at rest, at peace. And when it came time for him to live his final earthly moments—at least on that side of the cross—he died in beautiful peace, saying, "Father, into your hands I commit my spirit" (Luke 23:46).

Colossians 1:19–20 says, "For in him all the fullness of God was pleased to dwell, and through him to reconcile to himself all things, whether on earth or in heaven, making peace by the blood of his cross." This was the price for our peace, the blood of the cross. And make no mistake, there is *always* a price for peace. It's true when we seek peace as individuals, and it's true when we seek it as nations.

Whatever the peace you seek, it has been paid for by the blood of Jesus Christ. This truth is made manifest in his words to his disciples after his miraculous resurrection. "Peace be with you,"[17] he proclaimed as he held up his nail-scarred hands. "Peace be with you."

In 1908 Andrew Carnegie built what is now the famed Peace Palace in The Hague, Netherlands. It was the turn of the century, the beginning of a new millennium, and hope was in abundant supply. What would the future hold? Whatever the answer, *surely* there would be peace!

"The kingdom is coming!" theologians of the day declared to willing listeners. "It's just around the corner!" The utopia that man had always dreamed of was close at hand, it seemed. And it was within this paradigm that the Peace Palace was created.

But then came World War I, touted as "the war to end all wars." But clearly that was not the case. That first world war only served to initiate a second, as well as side-wars and rumors of wars galore. The end result of that entire century? The distinguished honor of being the bloodiest century in human history.

At this writing, we are in the early days of the twenty-first century. And still we face wars and rumors of wars all over the world. We can't settle on peace in the Middle East. We can't settle on peace in Iraq. There is, it seems, a lack of peace everywhere the eye turns, everywhere the heart ventures to roam.

One day a friend of mine who was visiting the Peace Palace had a brief conversation with a woman who works there. That staffer said, "In the library of the Peace Palace, we have every book known to humankind published on the subject of peace."

My friend, a Christ-follower and possessor of keen wit, said, "Fantastic! Do you have Billy Graham's book *Peace with God?*"

Her face flushed red as she admitted that they did not.

"Oh," he said, "well, *surely* you have a Bible in there!"

She thought for a moment and then replied, "Hmmm, I *think* so."

She halfheartedly looked around and finally found a Bible that had been stuffed on a back shelf in the far recesses of the library. In that moment as the dusty Book surfaced, my friend was reminded of what you and I both surely know: it is impossible to know the peace of God without God.

"Peace is a fable," a reporter for *The New York Times* concluded recently as he considered the ongoing wars we fight. And indeed peace *is* a fable, apart from God. To know peace—personally, relationally, globally—we must begin by getting to know the Prince of Peace, Jesus Christ. "*My* peace I give to you." There's no other peace to be found.

8

We Are Our Brother's Keeper

Real-Deal Disciples in a Fraud-Filled Age

In the wonderful wordless children's book *The Flower Man*[1] an entire town is transformed by the presence of one simple soul. Dressed in a frumpy green jacket, well-worn trousers, and a navy blue hat and carrying an umbrella in one hand and a tattered bag in the other, the Flower Man, an elderly man with hazel eyes and a gray moustache, crosses the bridge, walks past the gas station, the bar, and the bait shop, and buys a home in an unfamiliar neighborhood.

The collection of homes and streets is devoid of any color, and his house will require a bit of work, but the Flower Man worries not. He eyes the dim silhouettes of passersby and people going about their lives on the other side of open windows all around—a struggling artist, a bored man in a bathtub, gossiping teenagers, a wishing boy tossing coins into a fountain, and one person wearing black who appears to be a thief. But instead of despair the Flower

Man feels hope. *Just think of the ways I can impact this place for good*, his countenance seems to say.

The next morning, the Flower Man rises early to mow his yard, hang the crooked shutters straight, and give things a fresh coat of paint. Suddenly his entire corner is flooded with light. Color, energy, brightness are all around—all of this change in one swift day!

As days turn to weeks and weeks march on, each person who comes in contact with the Flower Man receives not only a freshly cut flower from his garden but also a friendly dose of "color" to carry with him or her—a listening ear, a word spoken in kindness, a simple good deed. Soon enough, as you'd guess, the whole town seems painted anew. The artist presents his canvas—a lovely work of art. The bathtub man now sings a melody. The snobby teens make an outcast part of their community. The boy by the fountain gets his wish.

Smiles now grace faces, laughter fills the air, joy returns to a joyless place—all because one person chose to care.

Some character traits can exist in you even when you're all by yourself. The personal fruit of peace, for example—you could be *perfectly* at peace with nary another human being around. (Perhaps even more so, depending on the folks who hang around your life!)

POWER POINT

Who has served as a "Flower Man" in your life thus far, someone who offered you an encouraging word, a friendly smile, a practical series of favors? Why did their kindness impact you so deeply?

But other traits require the *presence of people* before they really get fleshed out. The second cluster of the fruit of the Spirit—patience, kindness, goodness—are traits of that type. In my view, it makes the successful living out of them all the sweeter because, just as the Flower Man saw, when we are faithful to manifest godly fruit in our interactions with others, we please not only our God and ourselves but also the ones we have blessed.

Learning Patience from the Story of the Guy Found in a Fish

The Sunday-school version of the story of Jonah carries with it an obvious message: it's no fun to be found in the belly of a smelly fish. But upon further examination, I think there are more substantive lessons to be learned. Here, in our discussion on that difficult-to-practice fruit called *patience*, we'll take a look at two that seem to stand out. But first, by way of context, let's review the story.

"Arise, go to Nineveh," God had said to his follower Jonah. "Call out against it, for their evil has come up before me."[2] But Jonah didn't *want* to go to Nineveh. It was a pagan place filled with evil practices and people who probably wouldn't be excited to see him show up. So, rather than rising to obey God's orders and make his way to Nineveh, "Jonah rose to flee."[3]

Jonah boarded a boat with a slew of strangers and headed out to sea to escape the presence of God. But God would remain near. *Very* near, and with power and presence that must have given Jonah great pause. In fact, God "hurled a great wind upon the sea, and there was a mighty tempest on the sea, so that the ship threatened to break up."[4]

As Jonah's shipmates scrambled to lighten the boat's load and save themselves from certain death, Jonah finally admitted that he had been fleeing from God and that the storm was probably a not-so-subtle invitation from God to come back home. All who were aboard knew that their only option was to throw overboard their newfound pal, which is how a man named Jonah ended up inside a fish. The destination had been "appointed" for him, the Scripture tells us, by God,[5] which, personally, is an appointment I pray I *will never* have to keep.

143

After three days, three nights, and a whole lot of prayer, God finally released Jonah from his fishy confinement. He then made his request of Jonah one more time: "Arise, go to Nineveh . . . and call out against it the message that I tell you"[6]—and this time (no shocker here), Jonah complied.

Jonah ventured into the obscene land called Nineveh, sure that God would rain down harsh judgment on the heads of these people who so obviously deserved it. So he preached God's message to the Ninevites, telling them that God had had it with their evil ways. And then he sat back and waited for heaven's fire to fall. But to his utter disbelief, not a single puff of smoke could be seen. Instead, much to Jonah's chagrin, God sent *revival* to that town, and an entire city repented from their wrongdoing and came to believe in the one true King, and God forgave them.

Jonah was fit to be tied. "I knew that you are a gracious God and merciful, slow to anger and abounding in steadfast love, and relenting from disaster. Therefore now, O LORD, please take my life from me, for it is better for me to die than to live."[7] "How dare you be *patient* with them!" Jonah might as well have screamed. "They deserved your *wrath*, not your *well wishes!*"

God then says to a fuming Jonah, "Nineveh has more than a hundred and twenty thousand people who cannot tell their right hand from their left, and many cattle as well. Should I not be concerned about that great city?"[8] One hundred and twenty thousand souls were redeemed, and God had chosen a simple man with a simple message to accomplish the whole grand thing. Here's the first lesson I think we can learn from this text: God is *always* up to something bigger than what our feeble eyes can see.

God Is up to Something Bigger

This fruit of the Spirit called "longsuffering" or "patience" (Galatians 5:22, KJV, ESV) has been described as the willingness to stay cool and to stick it out until you arrive at the best possible outcome. It is *endurance* and *consistency*, the ability to stand firm in the Lord as you wait upon him, even in the midst of affliction. It's not passivity, it's not complacency, and it's not mere compliance. Patience, as Warren Wiersbe says, is "endurance in action."[9]

Two words in the New Testament describe this fruit. One is the word *hupomone*, which means "to stay under" or "to abide under." The other is the word I'd like to draw your attention to now. *Makrothumeo* reminds us of two concepts: "macro," meaning large in scale or scope (as opposed to "micro," which indicates something small or abbreviated) and "thermal," which refers to fire or fuel or heat. Put the two together, and you wind up with a long fuse, which is exactly what long-suffering means.

Our God is a God of long fuses. He is a God of patience. Various portions of Scripture tell us that God is a God of "endurance,"[10] that he is "slow to anger, and abounding in steadfast love and faithfulness,"[11] that we who are Christ-followers received mercy from God so that in us "Jesus Christ might display his perfect patience as an example to those who were to believe in him for eternal life,"[12] and that he "endured with much patience vessels of wrath prepared for destruction, in order to make known the riches of his glory."[13] Again, God is the God of the long fuse.

What's more, our God is looking for a few additional long fuses to join him in his work.

We Can Choose to Join God in His Work or We Can Choose to Quit

Clearly, God could have redeemed Nineveh without Jonah in tow. But what fun is that for the One who prizes relationships the most? The second lesson I think we can take away from Jonah's story, in addition to the fact that God is always up to something bigger, is that more times than not, that something bigger is wide-open for our involvement.

Each week I see Christ-followers make the choice to quit. "I'm so tired," they whine. "I can't take it anymore!" "I'm outta here."

They quit on themselves. They quit on their loved ones. They quit on their boss. They quit on life. They turn in their jerseys and shuffle on home. Sometimes it's financial pressure that causes their demise. Sometimes it's relational stuff that does them in. Still other times the issue is emotional or physical or occupational or, on occasion, all of the above. But regardless what the *it* is, they decide that because of it, their only option is to quickly jump ship.

Obviously, God would encourage a different choice.

Enduring with Ourselves

The danger with indulging the desire to bail is that the thinking can seep into our spiritual attitudes as well. An ounce of difficulty enters a person's equation, and he begins to question God. Answers to prayers don't come as quickly as a woman wants, so she ditches the practice altogether. A little hard work is required to help someone develop greater intimacy with Christ, and he says, "No thanks. If I can't be fully developed as a follower of Christ in the next, say, fifteen minutes, then maybe this religion just isn't the one for me."

P O W E R P O I N T

What thoughts or practices help you not to give in when life deals you a leveling blow? How do you keep from quitting when your personal circumstances seem to be saying, "Just quit"?

The idea of endurance is that we persevere in doing what is important, what is significant. We keep the commitments we made to God—commitments about trusting him with our roles, our gifts, our lives—so that one day we will look as much like him as possible. We will bear the marks of a fully devoted Christ-follower to a waiting and watching world.

The apostle Paul, who back in his day was the poster child for endurance, indicated at least two personal practices that must be adopted if we ever hope to learn to endure with ourselves, to not quit on the person whom God has created us to be.

Authenticity

In 2 Corinthians 4:1–2 Paul writes, "Therefore, having this ministry by the mercy of God, we do not lose heart. But we have renounced disgraceful, underhanded ways. We refuse to practice cunning or to tamper with God's word, but by the open statement of the truth we would commend ourselves to everyone's conscience in the sight of God."

In essence, what Paul was saying is this: "Before God and before you, I tell you that what you see is what you get. I am who I present myself to be. I am authentic through and through."

Paul understood that there is nothing more exhausting, nothing that makes you want to quit on yourself more than letting deception rule and reign over your life, especially when you're trying to serve the Lord. Covering up, hiding, hypocrisy, sweeping sins under the rug—there's no quicker way to kill off patience than to choose to live a lie. First and foremost, it takes *authenticity* to endure.

P O W E R P O I N T

Are you who you present yourself to be? Are you the real deal when it comes to following Christ?

Most people know where their areas of hypocrisy exist. Perhaps they judge others for indulging a sin that they too indulge. Or maybe they say they love God but refuse to love people. The list could go on. As you take a look at your own life, where are your pockets of hypocrisy, untended areas that are keeping you from being a real-deal Christ-follower?

Are you who you present yourself to be? Are you the real deal when it comes to following Christ? If not, renounce the disgraceful things in your life, and trust God to keep you from losing heart. As you learn to wait on God to grow you up and develop you in his image, you will have your strength renewed. Isaiah 40:31 promises that you will mount up with wings as eagles, you will run and not be weary, and you will walk and not grow faint. In short, you'll choose at all costs *not to quit*.

Acceptance

For the past decade or so, an interesting dynamic has unfolded in my life. I've noticed that people no longer walk up to me and say, "Hey, Jack! How are you doing?" Instead, with poorly hidden shock in their voice, they say things like, "You're looking good these days!"

What they really mean is, "You're looking good . . . for an *old* guy."

Anyway, I can now vouch for the validity of 2 Corinthians 4:16, which says, "Though our outer self is wasting away, our inner self is being renewed day by day." As I have evidently proven to some of my friends, we cannot stop the advancing of age. We will all face days when we're all too aware that our bodies are perishing. Our eyesight will fail, our knees will get stiff, and our muscles will cry for relief. But because of the work of the Holy Spirit in us, we can be made good as new every day. Now *that's* a beautiful promise!

Clearly, the type of endurance Paul speaks of in Scripture has to do with more than mere outward appearance. But for our looks-obsessed culture, that's a decent place to start. Accept the exterior God has crafted for you, my friend. Thank him for eyes to see, ears to hear, a nose that knows when the pizza has arrived. Bless him for each year as it goes by rather than cursing its effects. And then focus your attention on what *really* counts, the renewal of your inner person.

In 2 Corinthians 4:8 Paul writes, "We are hard-pressed on every side, yet not crushed; we are perplexed, but not in despair" (NKJV). Certainly this life can be perplexing. But while we don't have answers to everything, we can bank on the fact that God is up to something big. When you feel like quitting on the life God has given you to lead, take a deep breath and ask him what he's up to instead. "You see the bigger picture here," you might tell God. "Please reveal to me what I need to know so I will not lose heart."

At various points along his journey, Paul was ridiculed, he was put in prison, he was persecuted, he was stoned, and he was left for dead. Yet through it all he said in essence, "I've never once been abandoned, because my great God is with me." Clearly, he could have ditched that whole deal and headed back to Jerusalem to sell used chariots. But that's not what he did. Instead, he continued to preach the good news of the gospel, trusting that even amid the pain, God was up to something big.

"I have fought the good fight," Paul said at the end of his journey. "I have finished the course, I have kept the faith."[14] That's the long-fuse spirit God seeks to develop in us—patient, long-suffering, endurance through and through. Let's declare now that we will never quit on ourselves. God has unspeakably good things in store for us, things that will delight our hearts and bring him glory. May you and I be found faithful to see them through to the end.

Enduring with Others

It's one thing not to quit on ourselves, but quite another to persevere with the people all around us. After all, if you can be patient with your friends, your family members, your neighbors, the rude clerk at your grocery store, then patience *truly* has taken hold.

I think one of the greatest victories Satan ever achieves is the accomplishment of relational discord. He "prowls around like a roaring lion," 1 Peter 5:8 says, "seeking someone to devour." But "he who is in you is greater than he who is in the world."[15] You don't have to be defeated by the enemy. You can live in the victory that is yours in Christ.

If you've ever played competitive sports, you know there's something in the heart of a true competitor that just *refuses* to lose. True competitors cannot *stand* to see their opponents succeed and then gloat over them. Can I give you a piece of advice? Refuse to lose where your relationships are concerned. Practice patience at every turn. Why? Because when you endure the petty frustrations and inefficiencies and annoyances, you hand Satan a defeat. When you look past your need to have your way, to speak your mind, or to always be right, you declare to God, "I know you're up to something bigger than what I can see here. I trust you with this person [wife, neighbor, sister, son, colleague, ridiculously egocentric boss], and I trust you with our relationship. I give you space and time to move as you please, God. Have your way here right now."

POWER POINT

> In which relationships do you need patience the most? In those situations, what makes the practice of patience challenging for you?

One day our perseverance will be praised with rich reward. One day we will realize that it was worth it to exhibit patience in our marriages, patience in our neighborhoods, patience in our work environments, patience throughout all of relational life. One day we will see it was worth it to refuse to quit on people.

Sticking It Out with What Honors God the Most

The worst defeat in college football history occurred in 1916. Georgia Tech was playing a small-town Kentucky college called Cumberland, and Georgia Tech defeated them 220–0. Cumberland College didn't get one first down the entire game. It was a good old-fashioned slaughtering.

Near the end of the game, Cumberland College's halfback was carrying the ball when he fumbled and catapulted the ball across the field toward his lineman. "Pick it up, pick it up, pick up the ball!" he screamed toward the lineman, who turned toward the halfback who was sprawled out on the field and said, "*You* dropped it. *You* pick it up!"

You and I both know how it feels to be so far behind in the game of life that all we want to do is give up. Our motivation is long gone, our energy is sapped, and hope is nowhere to be found. But tucked behind those feelings stands the promise of Galatians

6:9 that we need not grow weary of doing good because "in due season we will reap, if we do not give up."

Billy Graham, now a ninety-year-old evangelist, can still fill stadiums with people who wish to know Christ, not because he's the greatest preacher in the world, but because he has been leading crusades since 1949. People come to hear him in order to have an encounter with God. But they also come out of respect for the perseverance of Billy Graham.

My pastor for forty-three years, Fred Swank, has led in the same way. To those of us whom he considered his "preacher boys," he always said, "Son, stay where God put you." It was an easy exhortation to follow because Pastor Swank had done just that. He lived the life God called him to live, steadily fulfilling his duty week after week after week. Those of us who planted our feet in his footsteps knew by way of his stellar example that sticking it out in the calling God gives you matters, and matters a lot.

I realize that you may consider *duty* a nasty, four-letter word. Plenty of people hold that posture these days and beg off their responsibilities by saying, "Well, I don't want to just do it out of a sense of *duty* . . ."

But what if Billy Graham had used that logic?

"Well, I would show up at tonight's crusade, but I don't want to go just out of duty."

"Yeah, I'd love to pray with that person who came forward to receive Christ, but I'm kind of tired . . . I'd just be doing it out of duty."

"I know I should read my Bible since so many people come to hear me teach God's Word, but I'm so busy today. I would be doing it out of a sense of duty, *so I think I'll pass."*

Fulfilling our duty is a God-honoring act on days when we feel like it and on days when we don't.

Ninety-nine Sunday mornings out of a hundred, I can't wait to get to church. I'm prayed up and revved up and ready to preach. I can't wait to see our congregation, to worship with them, and to join them in the presence of God.

But every now and then there comes a Sunday morning when I don't feel like going. I'd rather call Pastor McKinley, one of our other teaching pastors, and say, "David, you're on today! I'm going back to bed."

On those days I don't want to preach. I don't want to sing. I don't want to shake a single hand. If I *were* to show up, I'd want to just stand in the pulpit and stare at the crowd like some of them stare at me every weekend. If you've ever stood on a church platform during a worship service, then you know the look I'm referring to. It's the look that says, "Reach me . . . I *dare* you!"

But even on my bad days, I show up at church. Why? Because duty calls. And my duty—my obligation—to complete the calling on my life must trump my negative attitudes and feelings. In thirty-three years of pastoring churches, I've missed only two Sunday mornings, and both were due to illness. (One was for the chicken pox when I was twenty-four years of age. Can you imagine how embarrassed I was to know that our guest teacher told the whole congregation I was home in bed with a kid's disease?)

My point is that when I am faithful to show up, God is faithful to show himself strong. "For when I am weak," Paul said in 2 Corinthians 12:10, "*then* I am strong" (emphasis added). God is my strength when I feel weak, and he wants to be your strength too. He sees the whole picture. He knows you by name. And he promises to be with you every mile of your journey.

On a foggy July morning in 1952, Florence Chadwick tried to swim the twenty-one miles from Catalina Island to the shores of California. She set out with her mother and her coach in a boat by her side, swimming a full fifteen hours and fifty-five minutes before she stopped and said she could not go on.

Interestingly, Florence quit swimming not because she was tired and not because she was cold but because, according to her, she "couldn't see the shore."[16]

After climbing into the boat and calling it a day, she was informed that she had quit a mere half-mile from shore.

POWER POINT

When was the last time you persevered in fulfilling an obligation that was especially difficult to fulfill? What emotions did you experience upon completing it? What aspects of Christlikeness were forged in your character as a result?

Three months later, on a crystal-clear day, Florence Chadwick gave it another shot. She finished the swim that time, and two hours faster than anyone had done it before. All because she knew how to "see" the shore.

Maybe you feel like quitting today. You didn't expect that life would turn out like it has, and you're wondering if you really want to try to pull yourself up again and keep fighting the good fight. Rest in the knowledge that God is up to something big in your life and in your calling. Prove yourself a real-deal disciple by allowing time and space for it to unfold. And then remind yourself that at all times, on all occasions, your God can see the shore.

A Cup of Kindness, Please

Last year I was in England, and one morning I headed out to grab a bite to eat. I saw a British man standing there, so I approached him with a smile and said, "Excuse me, but do you know where I might find a good breakfast place?"

With obvious disdain for Americans and a noticeable smirk on his face, he unapologetically looked at me and said, "Scotland!"

Kindness—it is a rare and cherished treasure.

As a little boy, I remember seeing a small sign in our Sunday school room every weekend that read, "Be ye kind one to another." That is from Ephesians 4:32, and it is fitting encouragement not just for children but for people of *all* ages.

P O W E R   P O I N T

What habits or practices equate to kindness, in your view? Do others consider you a kind person?

Be ye kind one to another—can you imagine if people really lived like that? At least one person who walked the planet did, and his name is Jesus Christ.

Kindness *Looks* **Like Christ**

Jesus was limitlessly kind. Whether he was wrapping up children in his arms, enfolding an outcast in community, easing the conscience of a sinner as he came to faith, or offering a healing touch to a leper covered in vile sores, he acted at all times with kindness. Still today, I think there is something a lot like Jesus that goes on when a person chooses kindness over every other course of action. Kindness looks a *lot* like Christ.

Several years ago in McDermott, Ohio, something incredible happened on a football field one Friday night. Kindness took hold of the game, and the result was truly a sight to see.

Northwest High School was playing their rival that night, Waverly High. Prior to the game, the two coaches talked by phone—not about Xs and Os as you'd expect, but about one Northwest player in particular. His name was Jake Porter.

Jake Porter was severely retarded, and although he had been on the football team roster for three full years, he had never once caught a pass, he had never run with the ball, and he had never scored a point. He participated in every practice and suited up for every game, but he had never played when the stakes were real and the stands were full.

Northwest's coach and Jake's best friend, Dave Frantz, had asked the opposing coach if it would be all right for him to put Jake in the game near the end and let him at least take a knee. "He can't handle a hit, but we're going to show him how to take a knee," Coach Frantz had said. "If it's all right with you, we'll put him in for the very last play."

Just before the game's last play, Northwest was losing 42–0. Coach Frantz called a time-out and jogged over to talk to the Waverly coach, and it was obvious a disagreement was taking place. Did Waverly want to fight for their shutout with real plays all the way to the end? Would Jake be denied his big moment?

A referee finally helped the two men settle the issue, and play resumed once more, *with* Jake on the field. The coaches' fight was really just a deliberation about how to get a running play under Jake's belt.

Jake had practiced taking a knee dozens of times before, but when he finally got his hands on the ball during a real game, he forgot what to do. He raced toward the wrong end zone before a line judge rerouted him the other way. As he ran his heart out for forty-nine full yards, the opposing team parted like the Red Sea and joined the Northwest players in yelling, "Go, go, go!"

As Jake crossed the goal line, the crowd went wild. Moms wept. Dads whooped. Players surrounded Jake and high-fived the young man whose life had been changed, all because one coach decided that not only should Jake touch the ball, but he should also score. He had told his team not to lay a hand on number 85 but instead to cheer him on. And that's exactly what they had done.

"Kindness is the language which the deaf can hear and the blind can read," Mark Twain once wrote. And I believe something in us resonates with kindness like that, kindness that communicates so much about us as individuals and about us as followers of Christ.

Kindness *Sounds* Like Christ

If you were to go to the doctor, and the doctor found a tumor in your brain, you would most likely want to know about that tumor, right? But what if the doctor said, "Well, I don't want to hurt this person's feelings by telling him he has a brain tumor. I think I'll just keep that information to myself . . ." You'd likely be outraged to discover this turn of events later.

The kindest thing that doctor could possibly do is to tell you the truth. Withholding the truth would be cruel. In the same way, we are called as Jesus' followers to tell the watching world the truth, but we are to do it with kindness to spare.

Sadly, though, that watching world often sees the angry fists of Christians rather than our tender and broken hearts. They often hear rage-fueled rants instead of soothing words of love. Of course, we will get angry over the things that anger God. But we must learn to express ourselves kindly. At every opportunity, we are called to be *kind*.

Recently my wife, Deb, wanted to go to a movie that she had heard about from some friends. I didn't necessarily want to go because from what I had heard, it was a major chick flick. And who wanted to sit through that when play-off baseball was on?

But I was working on this chapter on kindness and decided it might be a good idea to practice what I preach. So we went.

Ten minutes into the movie, which was rated PG-13 by the way, we were confronted with incredibly offensive language. Five minutes after that, an openly gay agenda was being promoted right before my eyes, and right before my heart. In good King-James English, I was ticketh off!

Deb and I eyed the couple we had come with, and all four of us left the theater. Did you know you can do that? They'll even refund your money, which I learned because I mustered the courage to approach the lady in the ticket booth and ask.

As I approached her, I realized the conversation could go one of two ways. I could either take a pious stand and berate her for the immoral movie she was showing at her theater or I could treat her kindly. I chose the latter.

The only way we are going to reach our lonely and dying world is to stand for truth in a gracious and loving way. We must practice kindness, my friend. We must operate not with an angry fist but with a tender heart. It is this type of kindness that looks like love; it is this type of kindness that can lead to repentance.

POWER POINT

What does it mean in your relational world to give someone "a cup of cold water"? How does such an act mirror the character of Christ?

Jesus said in Mark 9:41, "whoever gives you a cup of water to drink because you belong to Christ will by no means lose his reward." So, how do we cultivate a little kindness in our lives today? How do we pour a cup of kindness for the thirsty ones we see?

Kindness *Tastes* Like Christ

While we can't cover every nuance of how to cultivate kindness in the few pages that remain, I'd like to touch on four distinctions that you can carry with you starting today.

The first way to pour a cup of kindness for another human being is simply to operate as a *comforter* in his or her life.

A Cup of Comfort

A man once was traveling from Jerusalem down to Jericho when vicious thieves pounced on him and beat him within an inch of his life. With zero regard for his plight, they stole his goods and left him there to die.

You likely remember how the rest of this story goes. A priest saw the battered and beaten man on the side of the road and

Everyone we meet is carrying an armful of burdens. Everyone we meet is having a hard time. Everyone we meet is fighting one battle or another. And therefore, we are to show them kindness, Christlikeness, grace. Speak words of life, my friend. The world has enough spirit-crushers out there already.

A Cup of Forgiveness

There is something about being forgiven that enables us to freely forgive others. Ephesians 4:32 says that part of what it means to be kind to each another is that we forgive one another as we were first forgiven.

POWER POINT

When have you chosen the path of forgiveness even though the other person didn't deserve it? How does it feel to forgive another person even when they seem undeserving of a second chance?

In Galatians 6:1, which shows up right on the heels of the fruit of the Spirit we're studying, we read that if anyone is caught in a transgression, we who are spiritual should "restore him in a spirit of gentleness." It is the kindness of Christ, when people fail or fall, to do all we can to restore them *gently*. Enough said on that.

A Cup of Generosity

The opposite of kindness is selfishness. This is the final distinction I'll offer as it relates to pouring a cup of kindness for everyone you meet: *be a giver*.

A member of our staff practices this in spades. Whenever he sees somebody standing on a street corner asking for money, he stops and hands some over. Whenever he sees a coin-collection container in a fast-food drive-through or on the checkstand of his local grocery store, he drops money in there too. He never boasts about this, you understand. It's just obvious to those of us who are out and about town with him that this is how he behaves.

One day I caught up with this staff member at church and gave him a good-natured ribbing about his giving patterns. He hemmed and hawed and diverted the conversation a bit, but then I said, "Listen, don't you know that you are getting ripped off with this giving thing? There are so many con artists out there, and who knows—the money you give the guy on the corner could be going straight to drugs or booze! Don't you think you should be a little more discerning instead of just throwing your money away?"

I was laughing and getting carried away with the whole conversation, but then this staff member looked at me and with a subtle grin said, "Pastor Graham, I know all of that is true. But when I 'throw my money away,' as you say, it cultivates the kindness of God in my life. I'm not as concerned about where the money goes as what happens in me when I give."

You know what? My colleague was right. *Nothing* will break the back of greed and selfishness like cultivating the fruit of the Spirit by being kind. Nothing.

One man wrote:

> I have wept in the night
> For the shortness of sight
> That to somebody's need I was made blind.
> But I have never yet felt
> A tinge of regret
> For being a little too kind.[19]

You and I both know that's true. Never once have we regretted being kind. Never once have we regretted clothing ourselves with compassion and kindness, as Colossians 3:12 encourages us to do.

If it has been awhile, then I challenge you to get up tomorrow and pull on those clothes. Choose kindness. Choose to be a comforter, an encourager, a forgiver, a giver. Pour a cup of kindness for every single person you meet.

Living
the Good Life

It is said that "the good life" can be divided into three stages. When we're little children, we're told to *be good*. We get a little older, and all that matters to us is *looking good*. Then we eventually reach my age, and our primary concern becomes just *feeling good*.

But really now, does all of this add up to the "good life" we seek?

Many of my contemporaries who admittedly are living far from God find themselves reflecting these days on the decades that have passed and asking the very same question: *What happened to my life?*

"It was supposed to be a *good* life," they say. "So many dreams, so many aspirations that just didn't come true. What happened to my marriage? It was good when we started, but now look at it. And what about my career? I was primed to take on the world, but it took me on instead . . . and won. It was supposed to be a *good life*, wasn't it?"

Unfortunately, my friends aren't the only ones feeling disillusioned in their search for the good life. For centuries humankind has been in pursuit of the "good" without "God," and in every instance they have failed.

Heathens ate and drank and were merry but in the end did die.

Moral relativists declared what was good or bad according to their changing circumstances and suffered degradation as a result. HIV/AIDS. Teenage pregnancy. The ordination of homosexual priests.

Hedonists took their stand for pleasure and in response were dealt a leveling blow. Internet porn. Pedophilia. Suicide.

So much evil. So much dismay. All because we have bought the lie that we can have goodness apart from God. "For what does it profit a man," Mark 8:36 asks, "to gain the whole world and forfeit his soul?" The answer, of course, is *nothing*.

The good life *can* be ours. But not apart from God.

Know the One Who Is Good

The Old Testament prophet Micah said that God has already shown us what is "good," which is "to do justice, and to love kindness, and to walk humbly with your God."[20]

Interestingly, if you get that third part right—"walk humbly with God"—the other two will come on their own. It is impossible to walk humbly with God in a consistent, heartfelt sort of way and not begin to take on his kindness and his goodness because God *is* goodness. He is the standard of goodness. He is the ultimate good.

Sir Francis Bacon once said that "of all virtues and dignities of the mind, goodness is the greatest—being the character of the Deity—and without it man is a dizzy, mischievous, wretched thing." If you have gone about the quest for goodness apart from the definition of goodness himself, God, then surely you relate.

Without God, we fall short, we struggle, we are good for a time but then fail—and fail in a colossal way if my slip-ups are any indication of what other people face. Human goodness can *never* last. But by the power of God's Spirit, the bona fide goodness, the fruit-of-the-Spirit goodness, shows up. We begin to know real goodness because we are endeavoring to know the One who is good. The good life, then, is the *God life*—the life lived in and for the presence of almighty God.

His Purpose

Throughout my journey I've caught sight of several indicators that tell me whether or not I'm living "the good life." For starters, I know I'm experiencing fruit-of-the-Spirit goodness when I am finding *genuine delight in the purposes of God*.

In 1975 I agreed to pastor First Baptist Church of Hobart, Oklahoma. I was a young pastor then as well as a young husband and dad. Deb's and my oldest son, Jason, was barely three years old at the time, and one day he and one of his friends from the neighborhood decided to spend the afternoon jumping on our trampoline. The other boy had on cowboy boots while he

Matthew 5:45 says that God "makes his sun rise on the evil and on the good, and sends rain on the just and on the unjust." Who but the One who is goodness would behave this way?

It is in God's good nature to give generously, even to those who breathe in his air and breathe out curses toward him. But even richer is his provision in the lives of those who love him in return. "What a stack of blessing you have piled up," Psalm 31:19 says, "for those who worship you, ready and waiting for all who run to you to escape an unkind world" (*MSG*).

God stands ready to give to you, my friend. Your God wishes to bombard you with blessing, if only you'll look to *him* for the goodness in your life.

His Plan of Salvation

Perhaps the truest indicator as to whether or not I'm living a God-given good life is heightened appreciation for his *plan of salvation*.

The ultimate act of God's goodness occurred more than two thousand years ago when he voluntarily parted with his only Son in order that you and I could be united with him forever.

The goodness we can know in life today exists only because of the sacrifice of Jesus Christ. We never could have achieved that goodness on our own, but at our point of deepest sin, God stepped in and gave us grace. It wasn't by good works of righteousness that we were saved, Titus 3:5 says, but according to God's mercy, by the washing of regeneration and the renewal of the Holy Spirit.

We enjoy powered-up goodness because Jesus endured the cross. And I know that I'm living the life he enabled when my gratitude over his gift soars sky-high.

One day a young man ran up to Jesus as the Master was setting out on a journey. The man asked, "Good Teacher, what must I do to inherit eternal life?"

Jesus would answer that young man, but only after clarifying one thing. "Why do you call me good?" he responded. "No one is good except God alone."[22]

Indeed he is. God is good. All the time, he is good.

Go About Doing Good

Jesus spent his entire earthly ministry doing his Father's bidding, and based on what we've just discussed regarding God, it will come as no surprise to you that if you were to condense Jesus' life into one simple statement, it would be this:

Jesus "went about doing good."[23]

Something very interesting happens to persons who are living powered up. They *go about doing good.* If you want to know how fully you are manifesting this fruit of the Spirit, scan your calendar for the last thirty days and see how often you simply "went about doing good."

When you saw a need, did you meet it?

When you heard of a problem, did you fight to solve it?

When you learned of someone who was despairing, did you rally resources to offer some hope?

George Small once wrote, "I read in a book that a man called Christ went about doing good. It is very disconcerting to me that I am so easily satisfied with just going about."[24]

POWER POINT

> Based on how you live your life today, would you say that you're
> more likely to "go about doing good" or more likely to merely
> "go about"?

The good life is not defined by the acquisition of toys or the vain pursuit of pleasure. The good life is defined by your proneness to let God's goodness flow through you to others.

Overcome Evil with Good

Whenever I recommit to live the good life, I find I have to remind myself of a caution that the apostle Paul offered to his apprentice Timothy in 2 Timothy 3:1–5.

> In the last days there will come times of difficulty. For people will be lovers of self, lovers of money, proud, arrogant, abusive, disobedient to their parents, ungrateful, unholy, heartless, unappeasable, slanderous, without self-control, brutal, *not loving good*, treacherous, reckless, swollen with conceit, lovers of pleasure rather than lovers of God, having the appearance of godliness, but denying its power. Avoid such people. (emphasis added)

People will be lovers of money, Paul says, abusive, disobedient, ungrateful, and all the rest. And somehow, based on what we observe in daily life, we read that litany and nod our heads thinking, "Yep, yep, yep, I see that happening, and that one, and that one, and . . ." until we get to the part about people "not loving good."

Not loving *good?*

Who wouldn't love good?

Isn't everyone looking for the "good" life?

But we live in a world where godly goodness is not always appreciated. In fact, in another translation that verse from 2 Timothy reads, "there will be . . . *despisers* of good."[25]

One of the high-school administrators in our community and I e-mail each other from time to time to check in and to offer prayer support for one another. He's a tremendous follower of Christ who overcomes incredible obstacles in order to live out his faith every day while working in the often tough environment of the public school system.

One afternoon he forwarded an e-mail to me that had been sent his way by one of the parents whose child attends his school. At the top of the e-mail my friend had typed, "This is what I'm dealing with . . ."

What followed was a scathing rebuke. The more I read, the more vehemently I shook my head at the cause of this parent's ire.

Evidently a small church near that school had offered to open its doors every afternoon and to let the high-school kids hang out in a safe environment and eat pizza. The woman was furious that this administrator had made the offer known to his student body and decided to let him have a piece of her mind.

The administrator was endeavoring to do good, and he was being blasted for it. There are *"despisers of good."*

I know my friend loves Jesus, but I also know he was tempted to blast back. That is, until a little verse of Scripture came to mind. "Do not be overcome by evil," Romans 12:21 declares, "but *overcome evil with good"* (emphasis added).

If you are single and are determined to live the good life by allowing the character of Christ to keep you pure until your wedding day, be prepared that there will be "despisers of good" in your life, at school, at work, maybe in your own family. They will despise the good you espouse, but rather than despise them in return, "overcome evil with good."

If you are a businessperson who has decided to hold up the value of integrity in your business dealings, I guarantee there will be some who despise your good. You may be put out of social circles, passed over for promotion, or preyed on by people who just don't understand. But I assure you that God understands. He sees you living the good life, and he plans to bless you in return.

When our Lord Jesus Christ found himself nailed to a cross, he made the difficult decision to overcome evil with good so we could be free to make that choice every day of our lives.

"As we have opportunity," Galatians 6:10 reminds, "let us do good to everyone, and especially to those who are of the household of faith."

Do good.

Have a passion for good.

Love good.

Live good.

This is the life that real-deal disciples seek.

9

Passion Fruit

Reining In What Seeks to Break Free

Imagine if you will two horses.

One is looking down with threatening eyes, stomping angry hooves into the dirt, throwing his head back, and twitching muscles along his spine, just daring anyone to come close. The horse whinnies and neighs and backs up suspiciously, snorting out defiant exhales and rearing up on his hind legs to let everyone around know who is boss. No one can get close enough to this horse to saddle him up; he's unpredictable, untamed, unsafe.

The other horse stands readily at attention. His motions are fluid, his gaze is undeterred, his breathing is steady, and his feet remain planted firmly on the ground. When his master is prepared to ride, the horse bows his head low, receives a friendly caress, and remains still while the saddle is fastened. Once on the open plain, he falls into perfect cadence as his muscles stretch themselves, his mane waves with the wind, and delight fills his eyes.

Two equally powerful horses, and yet only one of them exhibits the *true* test of power—self-control.

The powered-up life is a life of power *under control*. It is a life that renounces ungodliness and worldly pursuits in favor of surrender and submission to Christ. Getting it right in this regard means reining in the fruit of *passion* through faithfulness, gentleness, and self-control.

Faithful Where Faithfulness Matters Most

I went to an anniversary party last week for a couple that has been married fifty years. One thing I noticed is that after two people live together for five decades, they start to look eerily alike. This couple's eyes looked the same, their smiles looked the same, their posture was the same, the way they talked was the same. But aside from superficial similarities, they shared something else in common. As they sat shoulder-to-shoulder, holding hands like giddy teenagers and grinning from ear to ear, they shared the sweetness of celebrating having gone the distance with each other.

Current statistics show that most men and women will never experience a moment like that. Forty-three percent of marriages end well before the fifteenth anniversary, and one in three implode before even ten years. So, what is the variable that determines whether a marriage will last over the long haul or whether even *individually* we'll make it that long? It is, in one word, *faithfulness*.

To be faithful means that you are loyal, dependable, responsible, and true. It's the fruit of the Spirit that proves you keep your commitments even when the circumstances of life may change. It is unwavering, undeniable fidelity—to God, to your loved ones, to yourself.

First Corinthians 4:2 says that "it is required in stewards that one be found faithful" (NKJV), and so I thought it best to begin our discussion on faithfulness by looking at the direct objects of that fidelity. To whom or to what are we to be faithful? To answer that question, we must first look at our faith.

Faithful to the Faith

The book of Jude, verse 3, says that we are to "contend earnestly for the faith" (NASB). I love how Eugene Peterson conveys that thought in his paraphrase *The Message*. "Dear friends," his version begins, "I have dropped everything to write you about this life of salvation that we have in common. I have to write insisting— begging!—that you fight with everything you have in you for this faith entrusted to us as a gift to guard and cherish."

POWER POINT

> What does it look like for you to fight for your faith? How faithful are you to practice doing so?

"A gift to guard and cherish," it is called, which is an apt description. As Christ's followers, our primary aim is to live in such a way that those around us, as well as future generations, will be compelled toward faith in Christ. And I am convinced that as it relates to our lives today and our legacies tomorrow, more of us would be found faithful if we would only first treat our faith as a gift.

When I run into kids from our church's student ministry, I tell them to fight for their faith because that faith is a gift. One of those young men or young women will likely lead Prestonwood one day. What joy there will be for them in future ministry leadership days because they have chosen to be faithful today.

When I talk to twenty-somethings who are wrapped up in their college career, I tell them to fight for their faith because that faith is a gift. "Don't let a fool challenge your faith!" I say. "Stay strong and be faithful to what the Word of God has taught you. The fruit of the Spirit is *faithfulness*."

I meet with business leaders in our community and challenge them to fight as well. "Your faith is a gift! Treat it as such."

If you serve on a board or are involved in a ministry or organization, I encourage you to take your place in the fight too. Contend earnestly for your faith, never once forgetting that it is a gift from God.

There have been several headlines in recent years about spiritual leaders or business leaders experiencing a moral breakdown. They fail and fall, and their life is left in shambles, and we sit back and wonder, "How did that happen so suddenly?"

But the truth is, faithlessness *doesn't* happen suddenly. It is never a blowout but rather a long, slow leak. Cracks in character eventually cave in, and all of life implodes on top of them. This is why we are encouraged to *fight* for our faith. The verb implies active engagement, preparedness, readiness, confidence in the face of warfare.

Throughout history, the faith of Jesus Christ has cost many men and women their lives. And while it may never ask that of us, we are to fight as though the ultimate sacrifice were indeed required. "Be faithful unto death," Revelation 2:10 exhorts. We must fight for our faith until the end so that our churches, our ministries, our schools, our workplaces, and our communities see what sets us apart from the world.

Faith produces faithfulness, and so if you are a follower of Christ, if you have placed your faith in him, then faithfulness ought to be manifested in your life. Faith is the belief; faithfulness is the ethical playing-out of that belief. It is how you behave, how you make decisions, how you opt in or opt out of what God intends for your life.

Faithful to Your Family

As our children were growing up, I always made sure that when they began an endeavor, they were challenged and encouraged to finish it. When my boys were playing athletics, they knew that if they decided to start a season, no matter what else happened to come up, they were going to see their commitment through. "None of this quitting mid-season stuff just because things might get a little tough," I'd explain. "That's just not what we Grahams do."

One year our youngest son Josh had a major shoulder injury the summer between his junior and senior years. Despite pretty severe shoulder damage, he returned to play baseball his senior year, and after the season had ended, his coach pulled me aside and told me it was one of the most courageously played seasons he'd ever seen. Talk about words that warm a dad's heart! I was so proud of Josh, not just because he had opted to play that season, but because he had opted for *faithfulness*. He was faithful to the finish all those years ago, which served to set him up for great displays of faithfulness still today.

When families are faithful to each other—whether it's a husband to his wife, a son to his parents, siblings to each other—there is a shared understanding that a person's yes means yes. There is mutual trust. There is mutual prioritization of the family relationship above all other human relationships. There is mutual love and respect and tenderness and care. There is a common choice made day by day not to do anything that would harm the family or the family's name.

POWER POINT

Do you consider yourself a promise-keeper? What evidence would support your response?

Being faithful at home doesn't mean that you merely make promises; it also means that you *keep* them—promises regarding your devotion, your attention, your patterns of communication, your stick-to-itiveness. "A faithful man will abound with blessings," Proverbs 28:20 promises, and what a blessed house it is where faithfulness feels at home. Faithfulness in the midst of our families—this is one place where the fruit of the Spirit blooms brightly.

Faithful with Your Finances

In Luke 16:10, Jesus explains that faithfulness is also measured by the way we manage our money. "He who is faithful in what is least is faithful also in much," he says. "And he who is unjust in what is least is unjust also in much" (NKJV). In other words, if you haven't been faithful with money or material possessions, then who in their right mind would trust you with *true* riches?

P O W E R   P O I N T

> How faithful are you with your finances? Why do you suppose that God cares where we spend our money?

God will invest in us what he can trust us to use for his glory, whether it be large or small. Ironically, I often hear people speak of how much more faithful they would be with their finances if only they had more finances to manage. It's the equivalent of Tevye's *Fiddler on the Roof* plea: "If I were a rich man, ya ha deedle deedle, bubba bubba deedle deedle dum . . ."

"If I were a rich man," these disillusioned folks all but sing, "oh, how I would live! I'd be generous with my church, a benefactor to the world. Give me some Bill-Gates money, and watch me *give, give, give!*"

Do you know what you and I both would do with Bill Gates's fortune if we owned it? We would do with it exactly what we're doing with the ten-spot in our pocket. Because as Jesus said, if you are faithful in the little things, then you can be trusted to be faithful over the great ones. God gives most of us about as much as he can trust us with. So may God help us to be faithful in our giving, especially as it relates to him.

What follows are three truths about giving to God. Whether you're new to the faith or have been following Christ for years, I think you'll find them helpful.

Give Spiritually

God established the biblical principle of tithing—giving the first tenth of any income we receive to the ongoing work of building his kingdom—as a spiritual act of worship. We do not give out of obligation or compulsion but rather from a heart of gratitude for all that God has done in our lives. He allows monetary resources to flow our way in the first place; giving a tenth back to his work reminds us of that truth.

Give Systematically

We are also to give *systematically*, not laying up in store but giving to God's work before we spend our funds on anything else. I'm convinced that many Christians want to give to God's work but don't for the simple reason that they do not have a system in place for doing so.

The next time you receive a paycheck or a direct-deposit receipt that reflects new funds having been added to your account, stop and tell God that before you write a single check against those funds, you want to be faithful to him. Ask him to give you the courage to write your *first* check to his work, preferably to a local church that is furthering that work.

Give Sacrificially

And finally, we are to give *sacrificially*. What good is it to give to the Lord that which costs us nothing? Surveys indicate that in the church in America today, Christians give less than 3 percent of their income to the work of Christ. What's more, studies show that the *higher* the income a person earns, the *lower* is his or her percentage of giving.

We recently established a new task force at Prestonwood that will encourage our members to invest in wills and trusts so we can continue the ministries of our church long after we are in heaven. Can you imagine what would happen if every one of us—not just Christ-followers at Prestonwood but Christ-followers all over the world—agreed to tithe our estates to the work of Christ and his church? Can you imagine the impact and the influence that act of financial faithfulness would have on future generations? We are going to walk by faith in this regard and wait expectantly to see what God will do. I hope you'll join us in that effort.

Faithful to the Fellowship

We are to be faithful to the faith, to our families, with our finances, and also to the *fellowship*.

The church is not only a place to strengthen beliefs; it is also a place to *belong*. Once we are in Christ, we are members of the same body. We belong to one another, and thus we are connected through Christ to the fellowship of the church. Hebrews 10:25 says that we are not to "forsake the assembling of ourselves together, as is the manner of some, but exhorting one another, and so much the more as you see the Day approaching" (NKJV). We are to *engage* with each other, and we are to *encourage* each other.

Engage with Each Other

To quote an old saying, "Some people only come to church when they're hatched, matched, and dispatched. When they're hatched we throw a little water on 'em. When they're matched we throw a little rice on them. And when they're dispatched, well, then comes the dirt."

But faithfulness requires just a wee bit more.

Faithfulness means that we actually *pursue* interaction with other believers. We *engage* in conversation, we *invite* folks into community, and we *expect* to see camaraderie take shape. Church is more than a place to hang out. It is a training ground for fostering relationships that honor God and sharpen us. This is why we have church membership. Membership offers a forum for accountability and authority that is unlike any other forum available. Sure, there is a time to visit. But there is also a time to drive a stake in the ground and say, "I'm in. This is the place I will call home. I'll be faithful to this place, to these people, and to the city we're trying to reach for Christ."

I am a church-man through and through, and I believe in the church of the Lord Jesus Christ so strongly that I have devoted my entire life to serving her. I want to be counted among those who are faithful to the fellowship known as the church. I hope that you do too.

What realities about your life and your church make it easy to be a church-man or a church-woman? What aspects make it difficult to fight for fellowship with other believers? Why might it be worth it despite the frustrations you face?

Encourage Each Other

In addition to engaging with each other, that Hebrews passage also says that we are to *encourage* each other.

As you grow in relationship to other Christ-followers at your church, be diligent about drawing out the best from them. Defend them in their absence, highlight areas in their lives where you can tell they are soaring, prompt them toward greater obedience to Christ and his values, and stand by them as a faithful friend. This brings me to the final area of faithfulness I see played out in Scripture, which involves being *faithful toward our friends*.

Faithful toward Friends

A contest recently held in England asked people to share their favorite definition of friendship. The top three winners, in descending order, were:

A friend is someone who multiplies your joys and divides your sorrows.
A friend is someone who understands your silence.
A friend is someone who comes in when the world goes out.

Similar to those sentiments are two verses from the book of Proverbs. Proverbs 17:17 says that "a friend loves at all times," and Proverbs 18:24 says, "there is a friend who sticks closer than a brother." If you have a friend like that, you are rich indeed.

In my line of work, acquaintances are many, but fine friends are few. A day doesn't go by that I don't thank God from the bottom of my heart for that handful of faithful friends who walk in when the rest of the world walks out of my life.

I want to be that kind of friend to others, not just receiving heartfelt care but dispensing it as well. May you and I both be known as faithful friends.

Staying the Course

The way to experience faithfulness is to experience the faithfulness of God. If you want to be faithful to your faith and to your family, to your finances and to the fellowship of believers and to your friends, then look long into the face of Jesus Christ who is *always* faithful and true. Study his actions and reactions, his conversations and his choices. "Great is *thy* faithfulness," the old hymn says. Indeed, we serve a faithful God. And because he never quits on us, we need never quit on life. We can be found faithful all the way to the end because, as Philippians 1:6 promises, "he who began a good work in you will bring it to completion at the day of Jesus Christ."

When the Scripture asks, "a faithful man who can find?"[1] I want to be able to raise my hand high in the air and say, "Here's one. Before God and others, I am a faithful man. I am faithful to the faith. I am faithful to Deb. I am faithful to our children. I am faithful to the church and to my calling to serve her. I am faithful to my friends." *That* is the faithful and fruitful life I want to lead.

I have never run a marathon, and I probably never will. But the people I know who do run them tell me it's a real rush. Jay Allison, a man in our church, frequently runs the ultra-marathon, which is a hundred miles long. A *hundred* miles, and all in one day! Whenever he updates me on his latest run, I look at him with the same pleading expression: *Why?*

Why would you sign up for the pain?

Why would you torment your body?

Why would you endure all that training?

Why?

I came across an article one time that was titled "Even Waddlers Need Marathons."[2] A sports psychiatrist in Washington, D.C. put forth a theory that if you live your whole life and never try to push beyond your personal physical limits, you'll miss something very important. Another psychiatrist chimed in regarding exactly what you'd be missing: "Discipline, learning to push through frustration, the joy of building self-esteem"—the list went on and on but finally concluded with this interesting idea: "Not everyone needs to run twenty-six-plus miles, but everyone needs to be a *marathoner*."[3]

POWER POINT

"Not everyone needs to run twenty-six-plus miles, but everyone needs to be a marathoner."

What "marathons" are you running these days? What motivates you to persevere?

A marathon for you may be finishing chemotherapy. A marathon for you may be pushing through a gut-wrenching challenge in your marriage. Whatever your situation, faithfulness declares that you won't merely start, sputter, and stop. Instead, you will finish well, going the distance for the Lord Jesus Christ and finishing the course as only the faithful can do.

We are not called to be *sometimes* faithful, not *when it is convenient* faithful, not *when it doesn't cost me anything* faithful, and not *when it's easy* faithful. We are called to be *always* faithful.

You say, "But, Pastor, I'm just not that strong!"

If that's true of you, then I have good news for you. God *is* that strong. And because of his Spirit's work in and through you, you can know that level of strength too.

I want to go the distance for Jesus Christ. At the end of my life here on earth, I want to be able to say, "I've finished the course, fought the fight, and kept the faith." I want it said of me as it was said of David: "after he had served the purpose of God in his own generation, [he] fell asleep."[4]

Let us choose always to serve our God with *faithfulness* in our generation. Be an always-faithful saint, my friend. It's a course of life you'll never regret.

Gentleness:
The Strength Subdued That We Seek

Prestonwood has a chapel on its campus that features nine ornate stained-glass windows, each of which depicts through signs and symbols a different fruit of the Spirit. When we were constructing that chapel, a woman in our congregation wanted to designate an offering to fund one of those windows, in honor of her husband.

She had been deliberating for several days and finally came up to me after a service one weekend and said, "I just don't know which of those windows to purchase because my husband has *all* of these qualities."

After I picked my jaw up from the floor, I thought, *What a wonderful thing for a wife to be able to say about her lifemate. What a blessed home life those two must share.*

In the end, the woman landed on the window depicting gentleness, the fruit of the Spirit we'll turn our attention to now.

The Manifestation of Gentleness
Several Christmases ago I gave my two sons a book titled *How to Be a Gentleman.* There's a shortage of gentlemen—and gentle women,

for that matter—in our world today, and I wanted to make sure they at least knew the basics of how to operate in that vein.

The book included helpful tips on how to use a knife and a fork and a spoon, how to open the door and let others go first, and how to exhibit common courtesy in the course of daily life. But while those practices are useful, they don't address the *real* proof of gentleness. Gentleness comes only by way of the Holy Spirit living and moving and acting in and through a person's life.

During the days when the apostle Paul wrote in Galatians that we are to be gentle, several cultural connotations of that Greek word existed. It was a common word that implied, for instance, the lightness of a breeze or the subtle healing virtues of a fitting dose of medicine. A breeze that gains speed and spirals out of control can devastate and kill. Certainly too much of a good medicine can ruin the person who is taking it. Similarly, gentleness—meekness—implied not weakness but *strength subdued*.

Bible scholar Albert Barnes defines this fruit of the Spirit this way:

> Meekness is patience in the reception of injury. It is neither meanness, nor the surrender of our rights, nor cowardice, but it is the opposite of sudden anger, of malice, of long harbored vengeance. Meekness is the reception of injuries with the belief that God will vindicate us. Meekness produces peace. It is proof of true greatness of soul.
>
> It comes from a heart too great to be moved by little insults, it looks upon them with pity. He that is constantly ruffled, that suffers every little insult or injury to throw him off his guard and raise a storm of passion within is at the mercy of every mortal that chooses to disturb him. The great heart of gentleness is strong in the face of injury or insult. It is the greatness and the largeness of the soul in which Christ is alive. It is living in peace and serenity and stability. It is the quiet confidence of knowing who you are and whose you are in Jesus Christ.[5]

What a beautiful description of the gentleness-led life—a life that quite frankly has rarely been lived.

P O W E R   P O I N T

What are your perceptions surrounding the word *gentle*? What life experiences have shaped those perceptions? How well do they square with God's exhortation that his followers be people of gentleness?

Only two men in the entire Bible are described as "gentle." In the Old Testament book of Numbers, Moses is described as "very meek, more than all people who were on the face of the earth."[6] Clearly Moses was not a weakling or a soft and spineless sentimentalist by any stretch of the imagination. This is the man who boldly and courageously stood before Pharaoh and shouted, "Let my people go!"[7] This is the man who led the children of Israel on one of the greatest historical journeys ever known, out of captivity in Egypt and into the land of promise. This is the man who, though he was great and powerful, was gentle through and through.

The New Testament profiles another gentle man, Jesus Christ, the Savior of our souls.

Jesus was born in obscurity and had very humble beginnings. He practiced a lowly profession, working as a carpenter until he actively ministered for three years' time. But he was a man's man in every sense of the term. If you were to have shaken his hand during those days when he walked the earth, you would have experienced the firm, callused grip of a person who worked diligently every day of his life.

In the early years of his adult life, my dad was a lumberman. One of his brothers was a carpenter, and every time I shook either of their hands, I was reminded just how rough those professions can be. They worked with wood and saws and nails and dust. But inside that rough exterior lived two very gentle men.

Jesus was that way too.

In the book of Matthew, we see Jesus introducing himself to people and inviting them to come join his cause. Instead of touting his power, authority, or greatness, Jesus spoke of his *gentleness*.

"Come to me, all who labor and are heavy laden, and I will give you rest," he said in chapter 11, verse 28. "Take my yoke upon you, and learn from me, for I am gentle and lowly in heart, and you will find rest for your souls."

Even during his triumphal entry as King of kings, Jesus let gentleness be his guide. "Behold, your king is coming to you, humble, and mounted on a donkey," says Matthew 21:5.

It was Jesus who wrapped up little children in his arms.

It was Jesus who paid attention to outcasts and put back together those who were broken.

It was Jesus who elevated the human experience by his very presence.

It was Jesus who put his arm around stooped shoulders that bore great shame, embracing them and welcoming them into the kingdom of God.

Rather than coming with a sword or with harsh religious rules, Jesus came to us as the good and gentle Shepherd. What a God we serve!

The Measurement of Gentleness

With every manifestation of Jesus' gentleness, we are reminded of how much growth we must undergo in the Christian life if we're going to truly be like Christ. So, how will we know when we're making progress in our pursuit of this magnificent fruit of the Spirit? Based on my understanding of Scripture, there are at least four litmus tests that help determine the presence of gentleness. See how you fare on all four.

Gentleness Respects All People

Gentle people are *respecters of all people*. This is the first test of gentleness, the ability to look past differences to see the common bond we *all* share as prized creations of God.

I have always found it interesting that the people we love the most are often the ones we treat the worst. Most men don't show common courtesy to their wives. In fact, these days if you see a man opening a car door for a woman, it's either a new car or a new woman. And women don't fare much better. They berate and nag and disrespect their husbands in front of their friends. Children are combatant with parents, siblings argue for their way, and harmony is seldom found. It stands to reason that we would have difficulty respecting strangers and new acquaintances when we can't even love our *own* clan well.

There's another end to this spectrum, though, which is that we treat those strangers and new acquaintances far *better* than the members of our family. Be honest now. If a movie star or a famous singer or the president of the United States knocked on your door, would you break away from whatever you were doing to receive him or her or would you say, "Hey, I'm busy here. Can you come back later?"

The truth is, you and I both would treat them with the utmost consideration and attention, even if we were rude and harsh with our kids or spouse just fifteen minutes earlier.

Scripture says that's a bad practice to adopt. "Do nothing out of selfish ambition or vain conceit, but *in humility consider others better than yourselves*," says Philippians 2:3 (NIV, emphasis added).

POWER POINT

How comfortable are you with considering others as better than yourself? What messages from society at large and from the media make it difficult to keep others in first place?

Considering others better than ourselves isn't exactly an easy task. But that's what gentleness demands. As Christians we are to possess not a demanding spirit but rather the gentle heart of God.

- Toward family.
- Toward friends.
- Toward strangers.
- Toward clerks.

- Toward assistants.
- Toward employers.
- Toward employees.
- Toward service providers.
- Toward the man on the corner who has no place to call home.
- Toward people of *all* shapes and sizes and stripes, every single day.

For eight years, President Ronald Reagan was the most powerful man on the planet. As leader of the free world, he possessed authority and control you and I will never fully understand. Shortly after an assassination attempt was made on his life, president Reagan was recouping in a hospital in Washington, D.C. He had moved from his bed to the restroom and minutes later could be heard banging things around behind the closed bathroom door.

Immediately an aide rushed in to check on the president, and when the assistant opened the door, he saw President Reagan down on all fours with wads of paper towels in both hands, mopping up some water he had spilled.

"Mr. President, Mr. President," the aide said urgently, "please get up! You do not need to do that! We have plenty of people who can tend to that. Please, Mr. President, let's get you back into your bed."

In his indomitable style, the president turned toward the aide and said simply, "Well, I made the mess. I can certainly clean it up!"

Strength subdued—*that* is gentleness.

The president could have popped off and bossed his aides around, but he chose a different course of action instead.

In my view there are two kinds of people. One kind walks into a room and says, "Here I am!" The other walks in and says, "There you are!" I wonder, which kind are you? A gentle person is considerate of other people and other agendas, never seeking to dominate, never focusing solely on self. As gentleness takes root in your life, you'll find yourself thinking about your issues, your problems, your situations, your needs, your wants, your cravings less . . . and less . . . and less.

Be a respecter of all persons, my friend, *gently respecting* each one.

Gentleness Restores Broken People

Galatians 6:1, which we looked at previously, says that "if anyone is caught in any transgression," we who are "spiritual" should "restore" that person "in a *spirit of gentleness*" (emphasis added). Every follower of Christ will stumble and fall and fail from time to time, but what a beautiful picture of the mercy of God it is when other believers surround that person with *gentle* love and care. You and I have received much grace, and we are therefore to *give* much grace away.

The word "restore" that Paul chose to use has to do with the medical process of the setting and eventual healing of a bone. That word always takes me back to my early years as a rambunctious kid. My mother never thought I'd live to see adulthood, I was so active and rowdy and crazed. If I *did* survive my own antics for that long, she wasn't sure that *she* could.

When I was six or seven, I used to roller-skate through our neighborhood. Typically, I'd grab my skate key (remember those?), and I would tighten up my skates as tight as they would go so that I could shoot down the driveway in front of our house and launch myself into a midair jump.

One afternoon, in addition to doing my usual jump, I decided I'd throw in a twist. I got the jump part right and the twist part right, but somehow I missed my landing. A little cement bump got in my way, and coming down with a *voump, voump, voump*, the full weight of my body slammed and bounced on top of my arm. Boy, did that hurt.

I slowly rolled over enough to see my arm dangling there, and all I remember thinking was, *I am not going to cry, I am not going to cry, I am not going to cry.*

I walked into the kitchen where my mom was standing and said with no emotion whatsoever, "Mama, I broke my arm."

As fast as lightning, my mother loaded me into the car, headed for the hospital, and rushed me into the emergency room, where X-rays confirmed that indeed I had broken my arm.

In those days, a broken arm warranted use of a terrible chemical called chloroform that acted as a general anesthesia. Evidently they had to put me to sleep in order to set the bone, but once I awakened, I boasted a big, beautiful cast on my arm. That made the awful chloroform worthwhile.

I thought about how I would ask all of my friends to sign my cast and about how girls would probably pay attention to me now and about how my teacher would probably give me a break from some of my schoolwork and about how I now had a ready weapon at my disposal, should anyone choose to mess with me, and about the myriad other marvelous things that could happen as a result of that cast.

About four weeks into my big-beautiful-cast-wearing adventure I was ready to be rid of that thing. I couldn't hold a bat, which meant that I couldn't play ball. Plus, the thing was itching like crazy. I stuffed a wire clothes hanger down in there, but nothing could take away the itch.

Finally, the day came when the cast was to come off. I was elated. Finally! Freedom from my self-induced prison!

After another trip to the doctor's office, a few minutes with a buzz saw, and a bit of advice about "taking it easy," I arrived back home, free as a bird.

Having nothing better to do, I grabbed my little red wagon and headed back outside. If you're from my generation, you remember resting a knee in the wagon and pushing yourself down the sidewalk with the other leg. Which is exactly what I did. Except that I did more than push. I *flew*.

You can imagine my surprise when I hit the very same bump that I had hit on roller skates and landed with a *voump, voump, voump*. Would you believe that the very same arm bore the weight of that fall? And on the same day that my cast had been removed!

That time I cried.

It's not that it hurt all that badly; it's just that I really did not want another cast. And I *surely* did not want another dose of chloroform.

Mama and I went to that doctor's office in Conway, Arkansas, and after receiving a sideways glance I heard him say, "Son, what in the world were you thinking?"

Suffice it to say, despite my begging, I was forced to endure another round of chloroform, another cast, and another six weeks of confinement. But as a result of those awful months, my arm bone was stronger than any other bone in my body. It had passed the test of endurance, and it had been set and reset, held and supported with gentle, loving care.

P O W E R   P O I N T

How does it feel to be treated with gentleness when you are feeling especially vulnerable? What does it reveal about the heart of God that his people are able to manifest gentleness when they are walking by faith in his Spirit?

It's a silly childhood story, but it drives home a very grown-up point. When a heart is broken, a life is broken, or a family is broken, God's people are to come along with gentleness and restore them to good health. It is *gentleness* that restores.

Gentleness Responds Quietly to Anger

Okay, are you ready for the third litmus test pertaining to the measure of a gentle spirit?

Proverbs 15:1 says, "A soft answer turns away wrath, but a harsh word stirs up anger." By intuition alone, you know these words are true. If you have ever had a little tiff with a loved one, you know that adding a rude response to the equation only makes matters worse.

People always ask me if Deb and I ever fight. To which I say, "Of course not. We *never* argue. We have discussions that can be heard several blocks away, but *argue?* Never."

Of course we argue. Of course you do too. But the key is what you do when an argument ensues. It is a *gentle* answer, the Scripture says, that will turn the conversation toward peace, toward health, toward usefulness.

That's true in your family, and it's true in your business too. You're in a business meeting and everybody around you is losing their head. Try being the one who is in control. Show calmness. Lower the volume. Ease up on the rhetoric. Listen more than you speak. Exhibit kindness even if nobody else follows suit. It is not the loud and boisterous tyrant who will win the day but rather the gentle giant who shows subdued strength.

In this life there will be disagreement. But when feathers get ruffled and temperatures start to rise, take a step back and show some gentleness. Then just watch God work. You'll be amazed every time.

Gentleness Relates Lovingly to Unbelievers

Perhaps the greatest test of gentleness centers on how we treat those outside the family of God. First Peter 3:15 says, "But in your hearts honor Christ the Lord as holy, always being prepared to make a defense to anyone who asks you for a reason for the hope that is in you; yet do it with gentleness and respect."

If you are exhibiting the other aspects of the fruit of the Spirit—love and patience, kindness and goodness—the day will likely dawn when someone will say to you, "What *is* it with you? Why are you so hope-filled and happy all the time?"

And in that moment, meekly, gently we are to give an answer for the hope that lies within us. Ours is a countercultural message, and unless we engage people with tenderness and a gentle spirit, we will not be heard. We will not win our generation to Christ by shaking our fists and raising our voices. We will never be able to outshout the darkness. But we can be heard. "You catch more flies with honey than with vinegar," the old saying goes. And as it relates to the gospel of Jesus Christ, we will compel people toward faith in him when we convince them that Christ's presence really can produce a gentle spirit.

Author Jerry Bridges says this on the subject of gentleness:

Actively seek to make others feel at ease. Be sensitive to others' opinions and ideas. Show respect for the personal dignity of the other person. When you need to change an errant opinion, do so only with permission and then with an extra dose of kindness rather than with a spirit of domination or intimidation. Avoid blunt speech and abrupt manner. Be sensitive to how others react to your words, considering how they may feel. When it is necessary to wound, also include encouragement. Don't be threatened by opposition, but gently instruct, asking God to dissolve the opposition. And do not belittle or degrade or gossip about a brother who has fallen, instead grieve and pray for his repentance.[8]

The gentleness of Christ is available to us all, if only we'll choose to walk that path.

The Outcomes of Gentleness

Above all else, the benefit of a life lived gently is that it pleases God. And as we looked at several chapters ago, our chief desire is to be pleasing to our Father in heaven. But in addition to his pleasure, a gentle life also yields other outcomes—namely, blessing, grace, and serenity in the here and now.

Gentleness Leads to Blessing

At the beginning of the Sermon on the Mount, as noted in Matthew 5:5, Jesus said, "Blessed are the meek. Blessed are the gentle, for they will inherit the earth."[9]

We tend to confine our God-directed wish lists to material possessions and good luck. But God says to the one who lets *gentleness* have its way, "The whole earth will be yours." Clearly, we don't understand the power of strength subdued. I don't know about you, but I'd like to give it a whirl.

Gentleness Leads to Grace

Gentleness leads to blessing, but it also leads to grace. When you obey God and submit your will humbly and gently before him, he will give you grace. First Peter 5:5 says that God resists the proud but gives *grace* to the humble.

Grace is his undeserved favor that requires no payment from us. Who doesn't want more of that?

Surrender to gentleness at every twist and turn in life. Let its effects worm and work their way through your speech, your countenance, your presence. And accept the gift of increased grace that as a result will be yours.

Gentleness Leads to Serenity

Gentleness also leads to serenity in life; miraculously, it produces *peace*.

The prophet Isaiah said that "in quietness and in confidence"[10] we will find our strength. When you surrender to a life lived gently, you simultaneously boost every other aspect of your life—your physical well-being, your emotional well-being, your mental well-being, and certainly your spiritual well-being.

POWER POINT

Who are the three gentlest people you know? What actions or reactions or attitudes contribute to their spirit of gentleness?

I have a friend who says to his children, "Calmness is the key to success in life." And I think he might just be right. If you can keep your wits about you when others are losing their heads, if you can roll with the punches when others take offense, if you can respond to insults and injuries with not harshness but grace, if you can showcase a quiet and gentle heart, you will definitely stand out.

Gentle people are exalted by God and admired by others. They are strong in character and commended by Christ. Indeed, there is nothing more beautiful than a life lived in full surrender to the gentleness so desperately needed in this world.

⏻

PGA golfer Greg Norman has always been known as a rather cold and impersonal force on the golf course. In various interviews he has explained that much of his hard-nosed demeanor comes straight from his father, who was also a tough man with a thick veneer.

"I remember when I was a boy," Norman once explained, "my father would return from business meetings and as soon as he'd disembark the plane, I would run toward him, wanting for him to pick me up and hold me. But my father held me off and would simply shake my hand instead. That's why I'm a bit standoffish," Norman explained, "as well as why nobody seems to know me out here on the tour."[11]

In 1996 Norman had the lead in the year's most prestigious golf event, The Masters. Going into the final round, he had a six-stroke lead over rival Nick Faldo, but he seemed to be losing his edge. Hole by hole, shot by shot, Faldo inched in on Norman's lead, and commentators began to speculate that Norman was choking for sure. In the end they were right, as Norman eventually was overcome by Faldo, losing the tournament, the title, and the day.

Sportswriter Rick Reilly later wrote of the event, "As Faldo made one last thrust at Norman's heart with a fifteen-foot birdie putt on the seventy-second hole, the two of them came toward each other, Norman trying to smile, looking for a handshake and finding himself in the warmest embrace instead. As they held that hug, held it even as both of them cried, Norman changed just a little. 'I wasn't crying because I'd lost,' Norman said the next day, 'I've lost a lot of golf tournaments before, and I'll lose a lot more. I cried because I'd never felt that from another man before. I had never felt a hug like that in my life.'"[12]

When people have lost their way, when people have fallen, when people have failed, when people have been broken, they need a gentle embrace. Jesus said that when we're lost or hurting or experiencing life's pain, we can run to him and be wrapped up in gentle love. May we be Jesus to someone today.

Self-Control
by Way of Surrender

One of the most sobering realizations I have made over the course of many decades of walking with Christ is that the biggest threat to my livelihood, the biggest enemy of my own soul, is not out there in the world somewhere. It's right within me. *I am my own worst enemy.*

On a near-daily basis I am all too aware of the "war against [my] soul"[13] that is being waged between the things of my flesh and the things of God. I understand the lament of Paul that we looked at in Chapter 3: "For I have the desire to do what is right, but not the ability to carry it out. For I do not do the good I want, but the evil I do not want is what I keep on doing."[14]

In all likelihood, you understand that lament too.

When I grew up in the 1960s and 1970s, the culture's constant refrain was, "let it all hang out." And let it hang out we did. But the freedom and joy that spirit of living promised was never delivered, and it's not being delivered today either. Everywhere we look, we see life being lived in excess. You know the list as well as I do: drug abuse, teen pregnancies, binge drinking, violent crimes, porn. We are a people living unrestrained, a people headed for disaster but for the ability to exhibit some self-control, courtesy of the Holy Spirit living inside of us.

Self-control is the achievement of power or mastery over yourself. *The Message* paraphrase describes this fruit of the Spirit as the ability "to marshal and direct our energies wisely." I would add that self-control is also the practice of regulating conduct and behavior according to the principle of sound judgment rather than the flightiness of emotion and desire and appetite.

Discipline of the mind, discipline of the body, discipline of the soul—self-control of this sort is to be the ambition of every Christ-follower so that laziness, selfishness, excessiveness, and extravagance can finally be overcome.

POWER POINT

In what aspect of life do you struggle most to exhibit self-control? Why do you suppose the "self" is so challenging to contain?

Whether you are trying to lose weight, learn a computer program, get better at playing an instrument, or tackle more challenging tasks such as breaking an addiction, ending an affair, persevering in prayer, or being content when circumstances bring nothing but pain, success in life comes down to discipline. Without it, life is aimless, reckless, and well beyond help.

But to exercise discipline demands a stiff price, because the excesses and indulgences surrounding us are so *alluring*.

Or so we think. Interestingly, our pet sins and worldly affinities don't seem so soothing and enticing when we see them as God sees them. In Galatians 5:19–21 (NKJV) the apostle Paul on God's behalf lists them in black and white: "Now the works of the flesh are evident, which are: adultery, fornication, uncleanness, lewdness, idolatry, sorcery, hatred, contentions, jealousies, outbursts of wrath, selfish ambitions, dissensions, heresies, envy, murders, drunkenness, revelries, and the like."

He goes on to say that those who practice such things will not inherit the kingdom of God. And we know he is right. We have dabbled in the list enough to know that a life out of control is a life of doom and gloom. It is the life of a loser, of one bearing zero fruit.

The apostle Paul often used athletic metaphors, and in 1 Corinthians 9:24–27 we find a powerful word picture of what it looks like to elbow your way past all the distractions and pursue godly self-control instead. "Do you not know that in a race all the runners run," Paul says, "but only one receives the prize? So run that you may obtain it. Every athlete exercises self-control in all things. They do it to receive a perishable wreath, but we an imperishable. So I do not run aimlessly; I do not box as one beating the air. But I discipline my body and keep it under control, lest after preaching to others I myself should be disqualified."

We exercise self-control, Paul says, not to have a *perishable* wreath placed around our neck at the finish line, but one that is *imperishable*. The commendation of God, the joy of knowing that we persevered faithfully until the very end, a legacy that boasts in Christ and Christ alone—these are the components of the everlasting prize we seek.

The Source of Self-Control

There's a great deal of talk today about self and the glorification of self. There is self-realization and self-actualization and self-gratification and self-expression and self-indulgence and self-approval and more. But God says that all of those versions of self must die. Galatians 2:20 says that once we are redeemed, we are "crucified with Christ" and that the only life we now live is the life lived "by faith in the Son of God."

For the Christ-follower, there *is* no life apart from Christ.

And yet week after week, believer after believer approaches me with several versions of the very same question: "Why does my life seem so out of control?"

In short, I say, it seems out of control because it is.

Self-control comes not by bearing down and gritting our way through serial bouts of behavior modification. Self-control comes by way of surrender. Wholeheartedly. To Christ. On a moment-by-moment basis.

As lovers of God, remember, the native air we breathe is the presence of the Holy Spirit. We inhale God's presence. We exhale our sin. We inhale God's power to be found more than conquerors in whatever situation we face.

This isn't rocket science, but as we learned from Paul, it does demand discipline—discipline to arrest sinful behavior mid-sin, discipline to allow God to come into the situation and redeem it, discipline to stay far from evil from that day forward. But oh, the joyous release when you realize you really are walking in greater and greater intimacy with the only true Lover of your soul, Jesus Christ.

I am helpless to control my own passions and my own appetites apart from the work of the Holy Spirit. You are too. But with his power in the mix, the self-controlled life can be ours.

The Specifics of Self-Control

Every aspect of life presents a battleground, where we will either surrender territory to the rule and reign of Jesus Christ or we will insist on controlling it ourselves. Because you and I don't have the ability in a single chapter to cover each of those aspects in turn, what follows is a list of six categories that tend to elicit the most intense fights—the words we speak, the thoughts we think, the reactions we allow, the pleasures we afford our bodies, the purchases we make, and how we choose to spend our time. First up? The tongue.

Taming Our Tongue

Behind those ivory bars you call teeth lives a beast whose name is the tongue. And when he is not brought under the control of Christ, he rages like a wildfire that devastates everything in its path. "The tongue is a fire," James says in James 3:6, "a world of unrighteousness. The tongue is set among our members, staining the whole body, setting on fire the entire course of life."

Pretty sobering words, I think you'd agree.

But words we know are true.

How has your tongue wounded another person? How has it blessed someone? What are the implications of possessing "a fire" in our mouths, as James calls it?

Surely you and I both know how it feels to be burned by the tongue of another. We also know what it is to burn someone else with our own.

But by the power of Christ, our tongues can also be used to *bless*. We no longer live in obligation to sinful ways, to slander and vile speech, to gossip and wrongful talk. We can utter *wholesome* things, *uplifting* things, *encouraging* words of life!

Just for today control your tongue. Ask Christ to redeem your words and to restore your desire for helpful speech. String enough todays together, and you'll craft a fresh lifestyle as it pertains to your words. What a blessing you will be to the heart of God!

Tracking Our Thoughts

You and I think roughly ten thousand thoughts a day. Interestingly, our minds are constructed in such a way that we can only think one of those ten thousand thoughts at a time. And after that another, and after that another, and so on and so on all day long.

What's also interesting is that each of those ten thousand thoughts serves either to draw us closer to Christ or to push us further away. Our thoughts ultimately produce our lifestyle because a thought produces a plan, a plan produces action, and action over time produces a destiny. What you ponder in your mind is what you will become. If we want to glorify Christ with our lifestyle, we must take captive our thoughts.

Billy Graham once said that you can't keep birds from flying over your head, but you can keep them from building nests in your hair. Such is the task of tracking our thoughts. They *do* fly and flit and chirp all around us, but we have some say over which ones land.

God has given us a wonderful capacity to think and to create and to dream imaginative dreams. None of these things is inherently bad, but when they soar through our synapses unrestrained, Satan can use them to wreak havoc. Second Corinthians 10:3–5 reminds us that the enemy of our souls stands ready to twist and pervert that which God intended for good. Don't fall prey to the culture's assault on your mind. Take that ground back by agreeing with Philippians 4:8: "whatever is true, whatever is honorable, whatever is just, whatever is pure, whatever is lovely, whatever is commendable, if there is any excellence, if there is anything worthy of praise, think about these things."

> Whatever is *true*,
>> whatever is *honorable*,
>>> whatever is *just*,
>> whatever is *pure*,
>>> whatever is *lovely*,
>>>> whatever is *commendable*,
>> think only on these things.

P O W E R   P O I N T

What people or situations or ideas come to mind when you read the following words?

true

honorable

just

pure

lovely

commendable

Tempering Our Temper

Metal is surprisingly brittle until it has endured the tempering process. But after being suspended in intense heat for a long enough period of time, it's unbendable, unbreakable, and firm.

In the King James Version, the term used to describe the self-controlled life we are to lead as followers of Jesus Christ is "temperance." We are to be tempered, like steel. We are to endure suspension amid intense heat so that we too will be unbendable, unbreakable, and firm in our stand for Christ.

Several weeks ago, I was trying to get back to Dallas after a road trip that Deb and I had taken to Waco, Texas. I was exhausted and anxious to get home, but I needed a couple of items from the grocery store before we could depart. I pulled into a supermarket, thinking I could leave the car running while Deb waited there for me, which would obviously shave precious minutes off the overall stop.

Inside the store, I grabbed what I needed and made a beeline for the express lane.

"I *love* it when a plan comes together"—this is the single thought I had as I waited in what was sure to be a very quick line. That is, until a few other thoughts crept into my mind. The clerk punched some errant buttons, and his register suddenly broke. He intercommed for backup support, while the rest of us stood there staring at his busted machine. Once it was operational again, the next customer in line wanted cash back, but the clerk didn't have the denominations she was requesting, and so yet again he was forced to intercom for backup.

I felt my blood pressure rise as I shifted my weight to the other leg and stared at the backs of the people who were standing lethargically between this time-consuming errand and my trip back home.

The next person in line insisted on switching out the bag of dog food he'd picked for another brand, and the person after that had more than the allowed ten items.

I fumed as I thought about how unbelievably irresponsible, inconsiderate, and obviously illiterate the rest of the human race is—"The sign says *ten* items," I muttered to myself—and then I thought about Christ.

"Oh, I am so sorry, Jesus. I was about to freak out here and blow my testimony altogether, all because of a ten-minute detour from my plan. Please forgive me. Help me be kind to these folks right now."

"Better a patient man than a warrior," Proverbs 16:32 says, "a man who controls his temper than one who takes a city" (NIV). Ah, how I needed that reminder then. And how I need it *every* day.

Training Our Temple

God has given us only one body for this life, and he has asked us to care for it as though it were a temple. Whether it's excess food or drugs or alcohol, I don't want to put *anything* in my body that I wouldn't be comfortable bringing into the temple of a holy God.

It has been said that six in ten Americans refuse to exercise. A greater percentage than that neglect patterns of healthy sleep. The epidemic called overeating has spread all the way down to the youngest children in our society. And I have to believe that at every downward turn, God shakes his head in disbelief over our lack of self-control.

"Your body is a temple of the Holy Spirit," 1 Corinthians 6:19–20 declares. "You were bought with a price. So glorify God in your body." We would do better to remember that price the next time we're tempted to give way to the abuses the world encourages that have no place in the Christ-following life.

Transferring Our Treasure

An area of life that sorely needs self-control is that of our finances. Mind-numbing amounts of debt, excessive spending, poor judgment, the lack of discipline—where money is concerned, far too many Christ-followers are failing the test.

Allow me to offer a few questions that serve as a filter as to which purchases should get made and which should not.

First, ask, "God, when is enough enough for me?"

And then, "Do I actually need this, or am I purchasing it because of an emotional impulse?" And, "Will this purchase further your kingdom or your goals for me as a follower of yours?" And, "Is my motive for purchasing it pure?"

Let the Word of God teach you in regard to issues of money management. The abundant life he offers cannot be lived under the heavy burden of debt and disproportionate spending.

Trading Our Time

"This is the day that the LORD has made; let us rejoice and be glad in it." We probably know those words from Psalm 118:24 by heart, and yet I wonder how often we live by them. Thomas Edison once said that time is the only capital that any human being has, and the only thing he cannot afford to lose. Indeed, our time is short. We only have today, and there are no guarantees even on that.

The last two years proved to be one of the most difficult and taxing seasons of ministry I have ever known. Our church launched another building campaign, we completed the build-out of a school that is housed on our main campus, we endeavored to up the ante on the leadership development of hundreds of staff members, we worked to disciple more than twenty-five thousand people who call Prestonwood home, I finished my second term as president of the Southern Baptist Convention, I fulfilled travel commitments and speaking obligations and conference appearances, and I would come home each time to the realization that I was still a husband, a father, a friend.

Don't get me wrong—I love my life! But sometimes the tasks at hand seem to outnumber the available hours in which to accomplish them. Have you ever had that feeling? The truth is, you and I both have the exact same number of minutes in a day, and the same number of days each year. And God has called us to be faithful with each and every one.

Here are three practices that have helped me immensely in my quest to surrender my calendar to Christ.

Be Organized

For many years now, I have kept in mind a reminder of what is *really* important. Getting my oil changed, cleaning out my files, and renewing my annual subscription to *Golf Digest* are all fine and worthwhile things. But according to the priorities of Scripture, I am *first* to seek the kingdom of God. And as I approach my day each morning, I find it extremely helpful to keep this truth in mind.

Organize yourself according to seeking God's kingdom first. Matthew 6:33 promises that when we are faithful to tend to the work of God, he will be faithful to cause everything else to fall into place according to his very good plans for our lives.

Do what is before you to do, and do it all for the glory of God.

Keep Your Promises

If you say you're going to do something, stay sensitive enough to your conscience to actually get it done. If you say you'll show, then show. If you say you'll pray, then pray. If you say you'll see something through, then see it through. Self-control has a lot to do with remaining accountable to the words you speak and the promises you make. A life in control is a life in which yes means yes.

P O W E R   P O I N T

Why does it matter that Christ's followers are people of their word?

In a similar vein, I'll share with you what I share with my staff members each time they stroll in fifteen minutes after a meeting's start time. "If you can't be on time, be early."

Do you know how much time people waste by running their life all the way to the margins? They have no white space in their day, no breathing room, no latitude should something unforeseen crop up.

Follow through on your word. Always be on time. And finally, watch for opportunities to serve.

Part of what it means to be a Christ-follower is agreeing with our Savior Jesus that we are here not *to be served* but *to serve*. Keeping your commitment to God involves keeping your commitment to serve. Welcome the responsibility to serve others, my friend, and you will sense the undeniable pleasure of God.

I don't want to spend my life treading water. I want to do something that *matters* with my days. If that's true for you too, then look for ways to squeeze some service out of the mundane tasks of your day. Speak a timely word. Commit an act of kindness. Offer to pray for someone who is hurting—and then do so right then and there!

We all have time enough to do what God wants us to do every single day that we are alive. Glorify him with this most precious of commodities, and watch your satisfaction level soar.

Seek God, Not Cheap Thrills
If there is one time-waster that trumps all others, it is this: too many Christ-followers are looking to be entertained instead of being content in Jesus Christ.

Have you ever considered how much time gets frittered away in front of the TV, the computer, a movie screen, or a video-game console?

We think we're desperate for entertainment, but our heart's real craving is for Christ. My advice to people who feel like their lives are out of control is to carve out time to experience God—in nature, in a mind-expanding book, in the quiet of an hour spent in solitude.

The Christ-following life is the most exhilarating, energizing, excitement-filled life there is. But it's a countercultural rush. It comes from the inside out, slowly, deeply, authentically easing its way on through us as we make God our primary passion pursuit.

10

The Empowered Church

*Christian Community
the Way God Intended It to Be*

Near the end of the second chapter of the book of Acts, we find believers engaged in two primary tasks. They are "praising God," and they are experiencing "favor with all the people." And they are doing both, Acts 2:46–47 says, with "generous" hearts, a root word that connotes the image of a sea without rocks.

At first blush, a rockless sea seems to have nothing to do with the healthy functioning of a church. But keep in mind these were a seafaring people living in a seaside community. Much of their time was spent on boats, and the best thing you can hope for on a boat is smooth sailing—sailing, as it were, without rocks. According to this passage of Scripture, church in the first century—church as it was intended by God, by the way—was an exercise in sailing atop smooth seas.

P O W E R   P O I N T

> Would you characterize your church experience to date as
> smooth sailing or rough and rocky? What factors do you suppose
> contribute to a church sailing smoothly in the will of God?

I don't know what your church experience to date has been, but I have counseled enough Christ-followers over the years to know that for many people, smooth sailing is not exactly how they would characterize church. Frustrated churchgoers sit in my office, shaking their heads in disbelief over the dysfunction played out in the churches they attend, wondering aloud if "healthy church" really is possible.

They read that Acts 2 passage and just grow more perplexed. How come *their* church doesn't look anything like *that* church? They cross their fingers and raise a hope-filled wish and close their eyes real tight, but as soon as they head off to church the next Sunday morning, they realize with downcast hearts that sadly, nothing has changed.

To understand what our churches are to look like today, we have to study the original that God designed. But to see that original design lived out in our churches, we, as individuals, have to endure some pretty tough work because powered-up churches like the one seen in Acts 2 can only take shape when you and I live powered-up lives first.

When you and I focus our attention on the fueling of God's Spirit and live in anxious anticipation of his fruit being born in our lives, we become the beginnings of a powered-up church, a body of believers who want nothing more than to praise God and have favor with all people. We set the stage for a church that is winsome in its witness, caring in its community, giving in its patterns, and loving through and through. *That* is the church of which God dreamed. And that is the church we can have.

Let me draw your attention to four characteristics of Christian community the way God intended it to be, in hopes of your adopting a powered-up life and seeing it ushered in.

An Established Congregation

First and foremost, the empowered church is an *established congregation*. Acts 2:42–47 in *The Message* reads this way:

> That day about three thousand took him at his word, were baptized and were signed up. They committed themselves to the teaching of the apostles, the life together, the common meal, and the prayers.
>
> Everyone around was in awe—all those wonders and signs done through the apostles! And all the believers lived in a wonderful harmony, holding everything in common. They sold whatever they owned and pooled their resources so that each person's need was met.
>
> They followed a daily discipline of worship in the Temple followed by meals at home, every meal a celebration, exuberant and joyful, as they praised God. People in general liked what they saw. Every day their number grew as God added those who were saved.

At the beginning of that passage, verse 42 (ESV) says, "And *they* . . ." Who is "they"?

In this context, the "they" is comprised of those who have been born again, those who have been saved and who have begun to grow in their faith. The congregation was established by their membership and partnership in the gospel. They were established by their tie to Jesus Christ.

Everyone is welcome in the church and is invited to attend, but only those who have received Jesus as Lord and Savior can facilitate its empowerment. And that seems to be proving a problem for churches these days.

Across America as many as 70 percent of church members in Protestant and Catholic churches alike have no personal relationship with Jesus Christ. They may walk an aisle, go down into the waters of baptism, pledge their allegiance, and say they believe. But in terms of engaging in an intimate, consistent, and personal walk with Christ, their faith is futile. "Prove yourselves to be blameless and innocent," Paul said to the church at Philippi, "children of God above reproach in the midst of a crooked and perverse generation, among whom you appear as lights in the world."[1]

"Come out of the direction the world is taking you," he might say to us today, "and follow Jesus instead. Get off the broad road that leads to destruction, and get on the narrow road that is paved on the heels of Christ." Conviction of separateness, confession of sin, conversion of life—these are the divine marks of a follower of Christ.

God has made the first move. He has taken the first step. He has opened his heart, extended his hand, and called us to salvation. The rest is up to us. We either respond by faith or we shut him out. And with every faith-filled yes, the empowered church gets built. An *established congregation* starts to spread its wings and soar.

An Enduring Devotion

Secondly, the empowered church is marked by an *enduring devotion*. "They devoted themselves to the apostles' teaching," Acts 2:42 says, "and the fellowship, to the breaking of bread and the prayers." Let's look at each in turn.

Devoted to the Word of God

The believers in first-century Jerusalem were undeniably devoted to the Word of God. Apostles and teachers instructed believers in Old Testament truths and, according to Matthew 28:20, "all things" (KJV) that God had commanded them. They were faithful to *know* the Word of God. They were faithful to *teach* the Word of God. And they were faithful to craft an environment where people were called to *devote themselves* to it.

POWER POINT

Is your church devoted to the Word of God? What evidences do you see to support your response?

To know and to grow in the Word of God should be the purpose and passion of your life. It should be the commitment and the devotion of God's church. When we gather as believers, whether in small groups or large congregations, our focus must remain on God's Word.

"A believer should count it a wasted day," Bible teacher John MacArthur says, "when he does not learn something new from, or is not more deeply enriched, by the truth of God's Word."[2] *Every day* we should dig deeply into God's great gift of Scripture . . . *every* day we live.

Lifeway Research recently came out with alarming statistics regarding the dropout rate of young adults in church. According to their findings, seven in ten Protestants between the ages of eighteen and thirty who had gone to church regularly during their high-school years quit attending by age twenty-three. A full 34 percent of those polled said that even by age thirty they had not returned. Which means that one in four Protestant young people have simply left the church.[3]

When asked why they had left, the young adults who were surveyed gave a variety of responses. "I wanted a break from church," some said. "Church members are too judgmental and hypocritical," said others.

Still others responded with answers like "I moved to go to college" or "I'm too busy with work" or "I feel disconnected with church people" or "I didn't agree with my church's views on social issues or their political stance" or "I'd rather spend time with people outside the church."

POWER POINT

What other reasons might cause people to abandon fellowship with a particular church? What would cause you to consider leaving your church?

And yet remember that 30 percent of that initial population of young people continued to attend church throughout their twenties because, according to them, they realized that without church it was impossible to stay in vital union with God and without God it was impossible to succeed in life.

"Church helps me in the decision-making areas of my life," some from that group said. "Church helps me be a better person," others responded. "Church helps me get through difficult times." "I have never tried to live my life apart from a community of Christ-loving people."

Princeton sociologist Robert Wuthnow once said, "Unless religious leaders take young adults more seriously, the future of American religion is in doubt. And the proportion of young adults identifying with mainline churches is about half the size it was a generation ago. Evangelical Protestants have barely held their own."[4]

Entertaining our kids has little value in kingdom-building efforts. As a church, we must hold fast to our devotion to God's Word. And if a long-standing, empowered church is part of the legacy we wish to leave, then we must be faithful to teach that Word—passionately, consistently, unapologetically—to the generations coming behind us.

Devoted to Fellowship and the Breaking of the Bread

Early believers not only devoted themselves to knowing and loving God's Word but also to *experiencing each other's presence* on a frequent basis. "They continued steadfastly . . . in fellowship, in the breaking of bread," Acts 2:42 (NKJV) goes on to say, which implied the sharing of meals.

Believers in the early church did more than get together for an hour a week and check their spiritual to-dos off the list. They sought each other out. They shared meals together. They were "in" each other's lives.

P O W E R   P O I N T

Describe a typical week as it relates to your church involvement. How closely involved are you with your church and its members?

One of the most important investments you and I can make in the course of our everyday life is to intentionally engage with a group of devoted believers. There is something so sweet about sharing a meal and a long conversation—about life, about love, about the workings of God in the world. If it has been too long since you carved out time to enjoy the fellowship of the saints, I urge you to do so soon. Ditch your other plans, and join together with five or six lovers of God who can encourage you, embolden you, and build you up for the journey that lies ahead.

Devoted to Prayer

In the life of the original New Testament church, prayer was vital and essential. It served as the "slender nerve that moves the muscle of omnipotence," as poet Martin Tupper once wrote.[5]

If we want the One who is omnipotent to move in our lives too, we must be devoted to prayer. "Call to Me, and I will answer you," Jeremiah 33:3 says, "and show you great and mighty things, which you do not know" (NKJV). Make prayer not only your personal assignment for private times with God but the priority of *every* setting. Pray over your Bible study class, over your choir rehearsal, over your family meals and your business meetings. The God of the universe is inviting your input and perspective, your praises and adoration, your heartfelt yearnings and curiosities and concerns. And in return he is offering his presence and power each day. It is the holy exchange of prayer—our weakness for God's strength, our questions for his answers, our confusion for his clarity, our dismay for his delight.

First-century believers were not content to be transformed by God's truth. They also wanted to sense his presence. Surely you and I crave that same thing. Ask God to teach you how to pray. Ask him to ignite your prayer life with sparks of the supernatural so that you sense his presence. If you need a place to start, lean into the prayers of saints who have gone before us.

In many churches today, prayers are free-flowing and spontaneous, but in Acts 2:42 believers were devoted to "*the* prayers." That definite article means they were praying other people's prayers, most likely from the pages of the Old Testament. I challenge you to incorporate this practice into your prayer life as well. Intertwined with your free-form dialogue with God, offer up heartfelt passages from Psalms and Proverbs or from published prayers you find.

Enriching Participation

The third manifestation of an empowered church is *enriching participation*.

A pervasive problem in local churches today is that its members suffer from "in-self-alitis"—the *disease of me*.

P O W E R   P O I N T

Where do you see symptoms of "in-self-alitis" at your church? How might you influence other believers toward a more selfless posture toward God and toward worship services and ministry activities?

Christians turn into consumers and come to church ready to shop. "Did I like that sermon?" "Is that worship style for me?" "Does the pastor dress to my liking?" "Are the sermons short and sweet?"

The purpose of their attendance has more to do with satisfying preferences than with worshipping the one true God, and when enough of these in-self-alitis sufferers convene in one place, the church turns further inward, inward, inward, edging the work of the Spirit right out.

I'm not sure if you've noticed this before, but when your attention is focused only on yourself, it's difficult to reach others for Christ. This is the constant battle we fight—personally and as the church—to make sure that our eyes are fixed on Jesus and on the people who need him the most. May God help us adopt the same level of enriching participation that those early believers had so that one day people will look at our churches as a benchmark for Christlikeness.

Also in verse 42 we see the word "fellowship." We think fellowship is coffee and doughnuts in the hallway after a weekend worship service, but it runs so much deeper than that. The original Greek word for fellowship is *koinonia*, which means "to hold in common." And once you are a Christ-follower, you have *much* in common with other believers. Our fellowship, according to 1 John 1:3, is "with the Father and with his Son Jesus Christ."

As believers, we share a common Lord, and we share a common life. Far more than a collection of strangers or even a collection of friends, we are sojourners in the mission of Christ. We believe together, we are bonded together, and as a result we *belong* together, and thus we fulfill our purpose, we stand firm in our faith, and we fend off the schemes of our enemy.

Satan desires to disrupt and destroy the fellowship of God's people. But Jesus said that because of their union in him, his followers can be of one heart, one spirit, one soul, and one faith. The lifeblood of enriching participation is when we seek the good of our common community more than the satisfaction of ourselves.

It's for this reason that early believers were willing and able to freely give of their own possessions so that needs in their midst could be met. Maturity, unity, charity, liberty—my heart beats fast when I consider what would happen in our churches if words like these were true of us. What a radiant Bride we would be!

An Expanding Celebration

A fourth characteristic of an empowered church is the presence of an *expanded celebration*. Acts 2:46 says that day by day believers attended the temple together to worship God, to learn how to relate with him more closely, and to understand how to reach the world for Christ.

As a result of their consistency and their vitality—two things sorely lacking in way too many Christ-followers' lives today—this church reproduced. Acts 2:47 says that "the Lord added to their number day by day those who were being saved." Can you imagine the joy of seeing someone surrender to Jesus Christ every single day? It is possible, my friend, when we allow God to fuel our lives.

"Just look at how they love God!" onlookers must have beamed. "And how they esteem each other!" Oh, that the same would be said of our churches too. May God deliver us from being just super-organizations and mega-whatevers. May we be *the church of Jesus Christ*—an established congregation saved by the love and the grace of God, a people devoted to the Word of God and to fellowship and to prayer, participants rather than spectators, and celebrants of the expanding kingdom of God. When we are faithful to proclaim Christ, he will draw all men to himself. What a glorious day that will be!

I was watching the Dallas Cowboys play the other day, and the commentators were remarking about Tony Romo's ascension as our starting quarterback over the past few years. After his first season in that role, he sat down with head coach Bill Parcells just before Parcells turned over the leadership reins to a new coach.

In what would be his parting words to the rising star of the Cowboys, Coach Parcells said, "Tony, you're going to be a great quarterback, as long as you remember never to settle for *just good enough*."

That's a great word regarding football, but it's an even better word regarding faith. Believer, never settle for just good enough. The Holy Spirit longs to power you up for a life you haven't yet dared to imagine. Let him have his way in your heart. Give him ground to roam free in your soul. Insist on living the dynamic, empowered life you were born to lead. And together we'll triumph in him.

216

Afterword:
Careful Thought to Your Ways

There's a remarkable story in the first chapter of the book of Haggai about how God's people let his dwelling-place fall into a state of disrepair, even as they poured loads of money and resources into keeping their own dwelling-places up-to-date. "The people procrastinate," God fumed in Haggai 1:2 4. "They say this isn't the right time to rebuild my Temple, the Temple of God. . . . How is it that it's the 'right time' for you to live in your fine new homes while the Home, *God's Temple*, is in ruins?" (*MSG*, emphasis added)

God was frustrated with his people and with their procrastination, with their lack of prioritization for the place where they would come to worship him. He rebuked them for living far beneath their God-given potential, saying, "You have planted much, but have harvested little. You eat, but never have enough. You drink, but never have your fill. You put on clothes, but are not warm. You earn wages, only to put them in a purse with holes in it."[1] Then in Haggai 1:7–8 (NIV) God delivers explicit instructions to his wayward flock: "Give careful thought to your ways," he says. "Go up into the mountains and bring down timber and build the house, so that I may take pleasure in it and be honored."

The people were sobered by God's anger toward them. With contrite hearts they responded to his request and went to gather the materials they would need.

Later in the story the people of God became disheartened because of the size of the task before them, and so God—the same God whose anger only lasts for a season, Scripture promises—sent his prophet Haggai to encourage them. Verse 13 (NIV) of chapter 1 says, "Then Haggai, the LORD's messenger, gave this message of the LORD to the people: 'I am with you,' declares the LORD."

"*I am with you*"—those four simple words were enough to boost the people's spirits and rally them around their cause once more.

Many weeks would pass, but the people continued their labor, rebuilding and reworking the Temple of the holy God. They served diligently, knowing that this was the task that God had called them to complete and that he indeed was with them as they worked. When things got tough, rather than quitting they looked to the Lord who said to them, "Be strong! My Spirit remains with you. Be strong!"[2]

Indeed they would be strong. They would remember that God was with them. And they would complete their task.

You and I have spent an entire book looking at what it means to power up for life and all of its highs and lows by looking to the Holy Spirit of God. And here in the story of Haggai and the sometimes wayward people of God to whom he was called to minister, we find the central truth of powered-up living. God's commitment to be with his people and to give them his strength—promises of his *presence* and of his *power*—always trace back to his *people's commitment* to first give "careful thought to [their] ways."

It was only after God's people humbled themselves, gave careful thought to their ways, and then chose the path of obedience to God that they experienced life in all its fullness, tasting the fruit that is born only of the Spirit of God.

"Give careful thought to your ways," God told his people twenty-five hundred years ago. "Give careful thought to your ways," he tells us still today. "Think about what you are doing. Think about what you are saying. See things as I see them. Please, give careful thought to your ways."

> Give careful thought to what you expose your eyes to.
> Give careful thought to the ideas you entertain.
> Give careful thought to what you give your heart over to.
> Give careful thought to where you plant your feet.
> Give careful thought to how you spend your time.
>> And your money.
>>> And your energies.
> Give careful thought to whom you choose to love.
> Give careful thought to why you choose to love them.
> Give careful thought to it all—all of your ways on all of your days—because from that careful thought springs promises of God's presence and power.

You alone know what aspect of life needs your "careful thought" today. But of this I will assure you: when you willingly and joyfully surrender your ways to the One who created you and who loves you like you've never been loved by anyone else, blessing will surely follow you all the days of your life.

⏻

The book of Haggai ends with a series of divine promises, made from God to his people then as well as to us now.

"From this day on," God says,
> "I will bless you.
>> "I will take you.
>>> "I will make you like my signet ring, a sign of my sovereign presence.
>>>> "I have chosen *you*."[3]

You have been chosen for great things, my friend. May you never settle for caring more about what you eat or what you drink or what you wear than you care about walking in God's ways.

Procrastinate no longer—your powered-up life awaits.

Notes

Part One: Wonder-Working You

1. Lewis E. Joncs, "There Is Power in the Blood," 1899.

Chapter 1: A Swift Kick in the Dish

1. John 14:12, author's paraphrase.

2. Acts 1:8.

3. See http://net.bible.org/illustration.php?id=8657.

Chapter 2: A Profile of Powered-Up Living

1. Matthew 25:21, author's paraphrase.

2. See, for example, Philippians 1:1; 1 Timothy 3:8–13.

3. Psalm 111:10 and Proverbs 9:10, author's abridgment.

4. Second Corinthians 6:2, NIV, emphasis added.

Chapter 3: Breathing Native Air

1. See http://www.smu.edu/experts/pitches/breathing-research.asp.

2. John 7:37–38.

3. Isaiah 40:31, author's abridgment.

4. See http://www.cnn.com/2008/WORLD/asiapcf/05/23/myanmar/index.html.

5. See http://www.breitbart.com/article.php?id=080506191623.jmg5ogbt& show_article=1.

Chapter 4: Praying with Potency

1. See http://seattlepi.nwsource.com/local/359497_bus18.html.

2. Joseph Scriven, "What a Friend We Have in Jesus," 1868. Emphasis added.

3. Acts 4:28, author's paraphrase.

4. Martyn Lloyd-Jones, *Revival* (Wheaton, IL: Crossway Books, 1987), 220.

Chapter 5: Marching to a Divine Drumbeat

1. *Halley's Bible Handbook* (Grand Rapids, MI: Zondervan, 2000), 734.

2. From Matthew 4:19 and Psalm 101:6.

3. Hebrews 4:12.

Chapter 6: Speaking Wisdom's Words

1. See Matthew 10:5–16; 28:16–20; Mark 16:14–20; Luke 10:1–12; Acts 10:42–43.

2. Acts 2:40.

3. Baptism does not save but rather is an outward symbol representing an inner cleansing that takes place when a person comes to know and love Jesus Christ. When Acts 2:38 says to "repent and be baptized . . . for the forgiveness of your sins," it doesn't mean that baptism is required in order to be forgiven of one's sin. The Greek word translated "for" is a preposition meaning "because of" or "in lieu of." We use *for* in a similar way today. For example, if you saw a poster in the post office that said, "Wanted for murder," you would know that the person was wanted *because of* the crime. In the same sense, "for" is used not to denote a necessary ingredient for the remission of sin but rather as a natural next step to take as a result of finally possessing a pure heart.

4. Acts 2:21.

Chapter 7: Mind Matters

1. 1 Corinthians 2:16.

2. Matthew 22:37–39, author's abridgment.

3. See 2 Timothy 1:7.

4. Ephesians 3:18–19, author's paraphrase.

5. Matthew 22:39.

6. From Luke 6:32–35, author's paraphrase.

7. John Eldredge, *The Utter Relief of Holiness*, CDs, (Colorado Springs: Ransomed Heart Ministries), 2007.

8. C. S. Lewis, *Letters to Malcolm* (Sisters, OR: Harvest House, 2002).

9. James 1:2, NLT.

10. James 1:3–4, NLT.

11. John 15:11.

12. John 16:24.

13. Frances R. Havergal, "Like a River Glorious," 1876.

14. See http://www.usatoday.com/money/advertising/adtrack/2005-01-16-track_x.htm.

15. John 14:27, emphasis added.

16. Isaiah 48:18.

17. John 20:21.

Chapter 8: We Are Our Brother's Keeper

1. Mark Ludy, *The Flower Man* (Windsor, CO: Green Pastures Publishing, 2005).

2. Jonah 1:1–2.

3. Jonah 1:3.

4. Jonah 1:4.

5. Jonah 1:17.

6. Jonah 3:1.

7. Jonah 4:2–3.

8. Jonah 4:11, NIV.

9. Warren Wiersbe, *Be Complete* (Wheaton, IL: Victor Books, 1986).

10. Romans 15:5.

11. Exodus 34:6.

12. 1 Timothy 1:16.

13. Romans 9:22–23.

14. 2 Timothy 4:7, NASB.

15. 1 John 4:4.

16. See http://www.nationmaster.com/encyclopedia/Florence-Chadwick.

17. Luke 10:36.

18. Matthew 5:39.

19. C. R. Gibson books use this quote prolifically, but in all cases it is cited as "Author unknown."

20. Micah 6:8.

21. Psalm 23:6.

22. Mark 10:17–18.

23. Acts 10:38.

24. As cited in John Borek, Danny Lovett, and Elmer Towns, *The Good Book on Leadership* (Nashville: Broadman & Holman Academic, 2005), 61.

25. 2 Timothy 3:3, NKJV. Emphasis added.

Chapter 9: Passion Fruit

1. Proverbs 20:6.

2. Robert Lipsyte, "Even Waddlers Need Marathons," *USA Today*, October 13, 2003.

3. Ibid.

4. Acts 13:36.

5. See http://www.studylight.org/com/bnn/view.cgi?book= mt&chapter=5#Mt5_5.

6. Numbers 12:3.

7. Exodus 8–10.

8. Jerry Bridges, *The Practice of Godliness*, Chapter 15 (Colorado Springs: NavPress, 2008).

9. Author's paraphrase.

10. Isaiah 30:15, KJV.

11. See golf.com, April 22, 1996, at http://www.golf.com/golf/special/article/0,28136,1722139,00.html.

12. Ibid.

13. 1 Peter 2:11.

14. Romans 7:18–19.

Chapter 10: The Empowered Church

1. Philippians 2:15, NASB.

2. *MacArthur's New Testament Commentary*, cited on http://www.bereanbiblechurch.org/transcripts/acts/2_42-47.htm.

3. Cathy Lynn Grossman, "Young Adults Aren't Sticking with Church," *USA Today*, at http://www.usatoday.com/printedition/life/20070807/d_churchdropout07.art.htm.

4. Ibid.

5. Martin Tupper, English writer and poet; cited online at http://www.brainyquote.com/quotes/quotes/m/martinfarq158341.html.

Afterword: Careful Thought to Your Ways

1. Haggai 1:6, NIV.

2. Haggai 2:4–5, author's paraphrase.

3. Haggai 2:23, author's paraphrase.